Bruce Robertson has a scientific background and takes a scientific approach to philosophy. He has a BSc in physics and an MSc in astronomy and also a Diploma of Education. He worked at the South African Astronomical Observatory in Cape Town where he observed and wrote a paper on the black hole A0620-00. He then moved to New Zealand and did a variety of jobs in the areas of computing, outdoor advertising and teaching. Subsequently, he switched to writing about philosophy. He is married with two children. This is his fourth book on philosophy.

Bruce Robertson

# THE ROAD TO FREEDOM

A Philosophical Journey in
Search of Understanding

AUSTIN MACAULEY PUBLISHERS®
LONDON * CAMBRIDGE * NEW YORK * SHARJAH

A CIP catalogue record for this title is available from the British Library.

ISBN 9781035891122 (Paperback)
ISBN 9781035891139 (ePub e-book)

www.austinmacauley.com

First Published 2025
Austin Macauley Publishers Ltd®
1 Canada Square
Canary Wharf
London
E14 5AA

# Table of Contents

# A Brief Biography

G'day, my name is Bruce Robertson, and this is: The Pattern Paradigm.

People always want to know a bit of background about an author. Presumably so they can evaluate whether the book is likely to be well thought out or is just a ramble of disconnected opinions.

So, I thought I would introduce myself. I have a scientific background and take a scientific approach to philosophy. I studied physics and maths at university before going on to work in the field of astronomy for quite a few years. Later on, I decided that philosophy was what interested me most, so then I focused my explorations on the domain of philosophy.

So now, some 40 years later, this book is a summary of what I discovered.

Doing the research in astronomy taught me the intricacies of the scientific method. I also ran my own business in outdoor advertising which was quite an eye-opener as to how the world, and business in particular, operates. I did some secondary school teaching (maths mostly) which made me think about the communication of ideas. I also worked as a commercial computer analyst/programmer which led me to learn about algorithms and computer hardware and software.

I also did some third-year university philosophy papers from which I learnt that the proclaimed rigour and irrefutable arguments of Western philosophy were actually not so rigorous nor irrefutable.

I also married and have two children who give me anchor points in the world.

I have written three books; the first one, published in 1989, is *Rocks and Waves, an Image of Reality*. The second one, titled *The Pattern Paradigm or The Science of Philosophy*, was published in 2012. The third one, titled *Making Better Sense of the World* was published in 2019.

# Introduction

Welcome to the Pattern Paradigm and the philosophical journey I describe in this book.

The aim of the Pattern Paradigm philosophy is to create a model of the world that makes sense and to facilitate better decision-making.

Ever since I left my teens, I have been interested in philosophy. I wanted to know how the world worked and to make sense of it all. I read the writings of many famous philosophers, but none of them assisted me in making sense of the world. So instead, I read many books on sciences, from geology to astronomy and sociology to mathematics. All the while seeking to make sense of it all.

This book *The Road to Freedom* is a simple, logical and concise summary of what I discovered. It covers a wide range of topics starting from the separation of mind from matter, how concepts are formed ex nihilo and on… but you can discover those for yourself as you read the book.

In this book, I will be describing an original philosophy one that you won't find anywhere else. I hope to show that it is logical, rigorous and dynamic. I have given it the name: 'The Pattern Paradigm' (TPP).

It constitutes a paradigm shift from standard Western philosophy (SWP). It doesn't use any of the precepts or long words of SWP. Instead, it presents a framework of logical ideas that can be used to link many different areas of knowledge into one comprehensive and consistent whole. I tried integrating the ideas of TPP with those of SWP, but they just wouldn't fit. There was nothing in SWP that I found to be remotely useful, apart from a few noted exceptions, such as in the writings of Hume and Kuhn.

I have a scientific background and take a scientific approach to philosophy. I seek out the facts and then try to find the best theories to fit those facts. But presenting a paradigm shift from mainstream philosophy to a new and original philosophy was a daunting task. I needed to be confident that it was not the case that I did not understand mainstream philosophy but that at its depths it was not understandable; it just did not make sense. In this endeavour, I gained reassurance by the fact that I had once scored highly in an IQ test conducted by Mensa.

Despite what its proponents might claim, SWP, the philosophy that pervades the Western world and which is taught at universities is fundamentally and fatally flawed. Its claims to truth are no more than subjective opinions. It exists only in a fantasy world that has very little connection to the real world. It is time for a paradigm shift and a new approach to philosophy.

The book originated as a series of videos on YouTube with the first one published in July 2021. The name of the YouTube channel is 'Pirate Philosophy' (https://www.youtube.com/@piratephilosophy5404). (I called the channel 'Pirate Philosophy' to indicate that it was about philosophy but was detached from mainstream philosophy). The average length of a video was about 15 minutes. Subsequently, transcripts of the videos were posted on the website ThePatternParadigm.com. I posted the transcripts to the website as I know many people prefer their philosophy in a printed form rather than as a talking head. Each of the videos was a stand-alone mini-lecture and most of the transcribed videos have become the basis for a chapter in this book. The transcripts have been amended for a book format and have been adjusted, improved and clarified. One video that has been excluded from this book is the one in which I offered a

US$5000 prize for anyone who could identify a significant logical flaw or inaccuracy in TPP. The prize was unclaimed and its duration has since lapsed.

The structure of this book is that of a journey of philosophical exploration. It begins with some meta-philosophy, exploring what philosophy is and what one wants from any good philosophy. It then dives deep into the fundamental separation of the beginnings of mind from matter. From there it works its way through epistemology, decision-making, science, mathematics and on to a look at language, culture and ethics. All the while linking the ideas into a cohesive story. Then towards the end, it explores imagination, understanding, laughter, the magic of life, fantasies and finally freedom.

This book includes most of the ideas contained in my previous books 'The Pattern Paradigm' and 'Making Better Sense of the World'. It also includes some ideas from my first book 'Rocks and Waves'.

I claim that it makes better sense than any other philosophy currently available. Its score is considerably higher than SWP according to the criteria for a 'good' philosophy of self-consistency, comprehensiveness, accuracy, logic, explicitness and simplicity.

At the heart of the philosophy is the pattern identification algorithm described in Chapter 8 which shows in a rigorous and logical way how concepts can be created from nothing more than sense-data and a logical processor.

The book does not present any new or controversial facts nor does it rely upon the opinions of other philosophers, and hence, there is no need for references. While the words that it uses are commonplace, it does use specific meanings for some of these words, so I have included a glossary at the end. I have also included at the start of each chapter the thumbnail picture I used for the videos.

So let me be your guide on a philosophical journey of exploration and adventure…

# Summary of Chapters/Road Map to Freedom

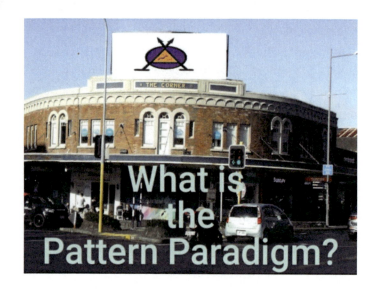

*I thought it would be useful before we start our journey to look at a map of where we will be going.*

### Chapter 1: Philosophy Is Important

Philosophy underpins so much of daily life that getting it right is important.

### Chapter 2: Is Philosophy a Paradigm?

Any cohesive set of ideas need clear foundations and processes for logical inference. Hence philosophy, if it is to be a cohesive set of ideas, must be a paradigm.

### Chapter 3: Is Standard Western Philosophy Naive?

The logic of standard Western philosophy is more hand-waving than rigorously logical, hence its claims of truth are naive.

### Chapter 4: What Makes for a Good Philosophical Paradigm?

This chapter discusses the meta-philosophy of what makes for a good philosophy: self-consistency, comprehensiveness, accuracy, logic, explicitness and simplicity.

### Chapter 5: How Does Standard Western Philosophy Stack Up as a Philosophical Paradigm?

Standard Western philosophy is evaluated according to the criteria of the previous chapter (SCALES). It is given an overall score of 3 1/2 out of 10.

### Chapter 6: Preparation for a Philosophical Journey

When looking to a new philosophical paradigm much of the baggage of what one might previously have assumed about philosophy needs to be abandoned. Then a few assumptions and foundations of a new paradigm are introduced: evolution and a logical processor.

### Chapter 7: The Deepest Depths of Philosophy

Diving into the depths of the primitive separation of mind from matter.

### Chapter 8: Patterns, Time and Space

Introduction to the logical process of pattern identification as the only possible process for how raw sense-data can be converted into concepts. An algorithm is used to highlight its logical process. A description of how the fundamental concepts of time and space can be extracted from sense-data using this process is presented.

### Chapter 9: Pyramids, Patterns and Why We Sleep

It is shown how the pattern identification process described in the previous chapter can be used in a recursive manner to generate a whole pyramid of patterns which constitutes a model of the world. It is noted that much of the processing for this is best carried out while asleep.

### Chapter 10: The Foundations of Reality and Purpose

A discussion of how the evolving logical processor introduced in Chapter 7 creates a sense of reality and the purpose of looking after its own physical body through the process of interacting with reality.

### Chapter 11: A Theory of Consciousness

It is suggested that one of the recursive patterns that is created at the apex of the pyramid of patterns is one that is associated with self-existence: 'I am'. In this way, the brain will have achieved self-awareness. It is further suggested that this experience of self-awareness is what creates consciousness.

### Chapter 12: The Logic of Decision-Making

The prime function of the brain is decision-making. An algorithm is suggested for the logic of this process with the aim of maximising happiness in both the short term and the long term.

### Chapter 13: Abstract Systems

A discussion of abstract logical systems that have no input from sense-data. It is shown how such logical systems can be created.

### Chapter 14: The Foundations of Mathematics

It is shown how basic arithmetic can be derived from a few rules of string manipulation. These rules are incorporated in algorithms which are able to conduct the operations of: +, -, * and / for any rational number. It further shows how elements of the abstract mathematical system can be mapped onto elements in a pyramid of patterns to create applied mathematics.

It is suggested that there are four main components of mathematics: pure maths, applied maths, creation maths (creating the mathematical abstract system) and pattern maths where mathematicians look for patterns in the theorems of mathematics.

It is further suggested that this approach to mathematics is entirely compatible with Gödel's theorems.

### Chapter 15: The Real Philosophy of Science

It is shown how the methods of science are an extension of the subconscious pattern identification process, described in Chapter 8, to a conscious use of such a process to create a more detailed model of the world. It is noted that the 'many worlds' hypothesis of quantum physics fails to meet the criteria of a viable scientific theory.

### Chapter 16: Words Are Labels for Patterns

Language is for the purpose of communication and its elements for this communication are words. Words are in essence labels for patterns.

### Chapter 17: Culture and Schisms

It is noted that while communication has many benefits it can also distort a person's model of the world and in this way can create discontinuities (schisms) in a person's pyramid of patterns.

### Chapter 18: Are Disembodied Statements Meaningless?

Language is for communication. Statements require a mind with a pyramid of patterns and a model of the world to interpret them and give them meaning. Hence disembodied statements which are mooted to exist independently of a mind (and despite them being popular in Standard Western Philosophy) are inherently meaningless.

### Chapter 19: Is Morality a Good Ethical System?

Morality as an ethical system is flawed in that it is entirely ineffective for those who do not believe in morals.

### Chapter 20: What Is Truth?

A theory for truth; what it means, how it is created and how it is used.

### Chapter 21: How Well Does the Pattern Paradigm Stack Up as a Philosophy?

The criteria used in evaluating the effectiveness of standard Western philosophy in Chapter 5 (SCALES) are used to evaluate the effectiveness of the Pattern Paradigm. It gets a score of 7 1/2 out of 10.

### Chapter 22: What Are Eleven Uses of a Good Philosophy?

Philosophy needs to be useful if it is to be meaningful. Nine uses of a good philosophy are proposed: making better sense of the world, understanding oneself and others, making better decisions, refuting erroneous claims, creating a personalised philosophy, achieving peace of mind, effecting psychological therapies, creating a positive attitude towards life and a guide to further philosophical exploration.

### Chapter 23: What Is the Logic of Imagination and Why Is It So Important?

Imagination is an essential part of the algorithm for pattern identification. For pattern identification to work most effectively all possible patterns need to be considered and evaluated before the best one is selected, this requires imagination.

### Chapter 24: Why Is Laughter So Important?

When a pattern within one's pyramid of patterns is re-evaluated, it can have a ripple effect on the patterns above it; a sort of mini paradigm shift. The realisation of new ideas often provokes the response of laughter.

## Chapter 25: Knowing vs Understanding

It is all very well to know the words that describe the world but what is important is to understand how all the nuts and bolts of the elements of the world fit together and function.

## Chapter 26: The Human Dichotomy: Fantasy vs Reality

There is a continuum between fantasies and reality. Fantasies have their place and uses, but we live in the real world. However, distinguishing between the two is not easy and constitutes a challenging dichotomy for humanity.

## Chapter 27: Where Is Freedom?

The brain is a decision-making device, and there are always choices; one has the freedom to make those choices and the consequences of those choices are real. So one needs a good model of the world to ensure that those choices have beneficial consequences.

## Chapter 28: Where Is the Magic of Life?

One creates a model of the world, but it is only a model. There are things beyond what we can ever know that give life its magic and mystery. These include: 'Why is there something instead of nothing?' and the amazing phenomenon of consciousness.

# Chapter 1
# Philosophy Is Important

*We begin the journey with a look at the importance of philosophy.*

Philosophy covers all aspects of life. Philosophy is important because it is akin to the air that we breathe. It is everywhere. It influences much of the way we think, the way we talk, our personal lives, society and politics, but even so, it can appear to be invisible.

It is important to test and perhaps adjust the assumptions and tenets of a prevailing philosophy to ensure that they are fit for purpose and are not simply adhered to because they are steeped in tradition and are too hard to change. For instance, if the prevailing philosophy is not accurate, in that it does not fit with the facts of the world and if it does not facilitate understanding of the world, then it can distort people's view of the world, and this must inevitably lead to problems.

Ideally, one wants a philosophy that is accurate and facilitates an understanding of the world, so that one can make better decisions and lead a better life. Also, one wants a philosophy that is irrefutable and cannot be undermined.

As such, philosophy cannot be left to professional academics who work primarily with words and try to avoid the deeper aspects of life; especially when they promote a brand of philosophy that is as naïve as SWP.

One example of an area of philosophy that particularly interests me and one that I think needs urgent attention is that of youth suicide, which ruins so many lives. It is not a psychological problem for there is nothing wrong mentally with these youth; neither is it a physical problem, there is nothing wrong with the body of the youth, and therefore, it is a philosophical problem, if only because philosophy covers all aspects of life. If nobody else deals with it, it is a philosophical problem. Perhaps the problem is that many of the youth of today have a distorted view of the world; they feel uncomfortable with their view of the world and dissociated from the world. Perhaps the underlying problem is that they have a poor or even distorted model of the world; and if that is the case, then it is a philosophical problem, and they are in need of an upgrade.

# Chapter 2
# Philosophy Is a Paradigm

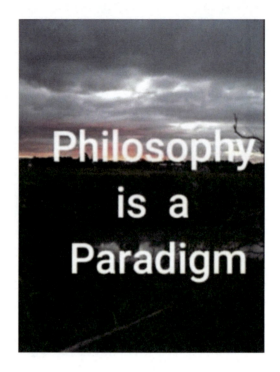

*In order to posit a paradigm shift in philosophy it is useful to first show that philosophy is a paradigm.*

So what is a paradigm? A paradigm in this context is a collection of ideas which have a degree of self-consistency and cohesion.

And what is philosophy? In this context, philosophy is a collection of ideas that link all other branches of knowledge into one cohesive and self-consistent whole.

Reality itself does not consist of words and ideas, it is only our model of the world that consists of words and ideas. All our knowledge of the world is but a model of the world.

Every idea or theory about the world is built upon other ideas. For any domain of knowledge, all the ideas need to be compatible with all the other ideas. This applies to science, politics, ethics and every other academic domain. In this way, they constitute a collection of compatible ideas, in other words a paradigm. At the very root of every paradigm are one or more assumptions; ideas which cannot be proven within the paradigm. Typically, these assumptions are implicit rather than explicit, for example, the presumption that the world is pretty much as we perceive it (naive realism).

In the domain of science, science is a paradigm as it makes assumptions about the physical realities of the world and then builds on those using logical inference. But science is not the physical world itself, it is a model of the physical world and as such, it is a paradigm. Even religion can be considered to be a paradigm because it makes assumptions; it makes assumptions such as there exists a god or gods. Religions that are based on such an assumption constitute a paradigm.

Philosophy is a paradigm for it creates a model of everything in the world. Yet the assumptions that are made for its foundations are typically not explicitly stated. They are instead implicit and are hidden within normative presumptions about the world. For example, one might make the statement 'the Sun is shining'. This requires the assumption that the object that seems to be shining up in the sky, is being correctly identified as being the Sun, and it also assumes that the receiver of the communication will use the same word to describe the same object up in the sky; these are implicit assumptions that are assumed rather than being explicitly stated.

Assumptions define paradigms. The assumptions that we make have similarities with the axioms of mathematics. In the same way that the axioms of mathematics define the system of mathematics, the assumptions of philosophy can also be used to define a particular philosophical paradigm. And of course, different assumptions will lead to different paradigms. So different assumptions in philosophy will lead to different philosophies.

The idea that a particular philosophy has a direct and perfect fit with the actual real world and is not merely a particular philosophical paradigm can be termed as 'naive philosophy'; for it is overly simplistic and naive. Reality itself does not consist of words or ideas, it is only our model of the world that consists of words and ideas. All our knowledge of the world is but a model of the world.

# Chapter 3
# Is Standard Western Philosophy Naive?

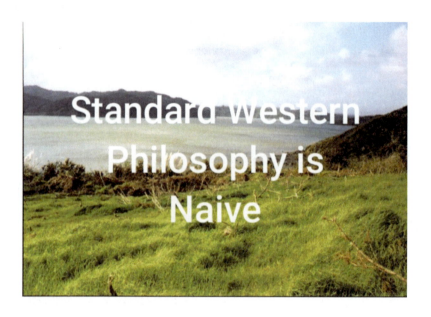

*Before presenting a new approach to philosophy, it is expedient to explore some of the flaws of Standard Western Philosophy lest people think that it is an irrefutable approach to philosophy.*

In the previous chapter, it was discussed how philosophy is a paradigm. In this chapter, I want to discuss Standard Western Philosophy (SWP) as a paradigm. In my opinion, SWP has a lot of limitations, contradictions and inconsistencies, and it is not a particularly good paradigm; and also has a number of aspects that I consider to be naive. Nevertheless, SWP pervades Western culture.

So what is Standard Western Philosophy? What do I mean by it? I mean, the philosophy that one might learn at university, the philosophy that one can read about in all the books in the libraries of universities; it is the philosophy presented by almost all philosophers that one might find in philosophy books. And what do I mean by naive? A naive theory or belief is one that is based upon surface appearances and which can be supplanted by a more mature theory or belief. So, for example, the idea many thousands of years ago was that the Earth is flat because Earth appears to be flat; we would now consider that to be a naive belief.

Science was naive around 2000 years ago when Standard Western Philosophy began. There were theories from Thales that everything was made of water. It had a certain quaintness, in the idea that water could be in the three different states of a solid, liquid and gas, it was a step forward. But today we would certainly see that the idea that everything is made of water as naive. The same with Aristotle's theory of gravitation in which he theorised that things fell to the ground because that's where things want to be. Again, we would now see that as being a very naive theory. Science has moved on since then; it has developed, and those beliefs of 2,000 years ago, have long been replaced and improved. Yet Standard Western Philosophy still has its foundations in the ideas of 2,000 years ago, with philosophy students advised to study Plato and Aristotle.

The problem with philosophy, as opposed to science, is that there are so few facts. One has to look at the internal structure of philosophy in order to determine whether it is a good philosophy or not; whereas in science, there are so many different facts and experiments that have been developed over time that the theories can be compared with the facts and if expedient to do so can be reworked and re-evaluated and improved upon. However, in philosophy, this is not the case.

So one has to look at the logic of philosophy in order to get some evaluation as to how efficient it is. One of the laws of logic within the Standard Western Philosophy paradigm is: 'if A, then A' meaning: 'if something, then something'. It is supposed to be obvious, and it is a foundational theory for SWP. But what does it mean? What is 'A'? What does 'if A' mean? Is it a symbol? Can it be used as a word? Is it an idea, a belief? Or does it refer to reality itself? Standard Western philosophers would say that it applies to reality itself. But then what is the correlation between the symbol 'A' or a 'word' and reality itself?

Standard Western Philosophy offers no logical connection between the two and if there is no logical connection between the two, then one can't rationally claim that it is a logical law; this is because it is not specific about what it applies to, and it is not even clear how it is to be used. A lot of the time, it is used in a non-logical way. People say things like, 'if it is raining, then it is raining'. But what do they mean by that? They go from a perception (it appears to be raining) to an actuality (it is raining), which is not allowed within a purely logical system for there is no logical process by which the transition can be made.

Yet that is the way it is used, and you might just as well say, 'the Earth appears to be flat', therefore, 'the Earth is flat', or 'the Sun appears to go round the Earth', therefore, 'the Sun goes around the Earth'. It is not logical; there is no logical process whereby one (it is raining) can be claimed to be 'true' but not the other (The Earth is flat).

So then one comes across the second law of logic: 'Either A or not A'. But again, what does this mean? What is it? What does it apply to? Does it apply to symbols, words, statements, beliefs, or reality? Again, standard Western philosophers would say it applies to reality itself. But then what is the connection between the symbols of that logical statement and reality itself? It is not logically defined. So it is not justifiable to claim that that is a law of logic.

On its own, the statement: 'Either the Sun goes around the Earth or the Sun does not go around the Earth' is meaningless; it says nothing about the world. It can only take on meaning if one of the two options is eliminated. But how can this be achieved in a purely logical way? The only way to do this is to use empirical observations which are not a purely deductive logical process. Therefore, one can't apply that particular logical law, to the actuality of whether the Sun goes around the Earth or not.

The second law of logic is often expanded into the idea that every statement is either 'true' or 'false'. It may seem to be logical, but then how does one determine whether a statement is actually 'true' or 'false'? There is no logical process for determining whether a particular real-life situation is 'true' or 'false' nor whether a particular statement is 'true' or 'false'; therefore it cannot be a part of logic that 'every statement is either true or false.' All that one is left with is a sort of hand-waving opinion about whether statements are 'true' or 'false'.

That is one of the problems with Standard Western Philosophy, a lot of the logical reasoning is missing, if it exists at all. The result is that one is left with nothing more than an opinion. And what is an opinion? An opinion is an idea that one has in one head and that one puts out for other people to consider, but it is not one for which the logical processes or foundations are clearly stated or clearly shown, or can be followed by other people. Most standard Western philosophy can be considered to be opinion, for it is bereft of explicit foundations and explicit processes of inference.

Standard Western Philosophy focuses on language: statements, propositions, justifications, judgments; that sort of thing. But they are all part of opinions, there is nothing particularly logical about it; other people cannot follow the particular line of reasoning that it supposedly has and so cannot recreate the conclusion for themselves. Take, for example, SWP's major tenet: 'knowledge is justified true belief'. What does that mean? All that it is doing is defining one word in terms of other words, and that is a job that is best left to lexicographers.

If one wants to try to define knowledge more precisely and if one does put it in terms of 'justified true belief' (or perhaps just 'true belief'), there needs to be a process by which it can be evaluated, to determine whether something is 'justified', whether it is 'true' and whether it is a 'belief'. Yet none of those can be achieved in Standard Western Philosophy without the inclusion of a hidden opinion or hand-waving argument. So one can only conclude that the assertion that 'knowledge is justified true belief' is itself entirely unjustified and hence to assert it as being meaningful or logical is naive.

The focus on language and 'truth' by Standard Western Philosophy also leads to linguistic tangles when they try to determine whether particular statements are 'true' or 'false'. For example, in the paradox of the Ship of Theseus, where a particular ship is, over time, repaired by replacing parts until eventually every bit of it is replaced. The question is then asked: 'Is the ship still the 'same' ship as it was originally? Or the paradox of the heap: If one has a heap of rice, and then one says something like: 'it is a heap of rice', and then one removes just one grain of rice; is it still a heap? If one keeps removing grains of rice until there is just one grain left? Is that still a heap?

At what stage does it change (if at all)? There is no philosophical answer to that. If it is a problem it is not a philosophical one; it is just a problem of language and labelling. Whether to label the mound of rice as a 'heap' or 'not-a-heap' is best left to lexicographers. It is naive to consider that it is a problem for philosophy or philosophers. Yet Standard Western Philosophy considers it to be a problem, presumably because they consider that language is a receptacle for 'truth' and every statement must necessarily be either 'true' or 'false.'

But this is only in a fantasy world. In the real world it makes no difference whether someone claims that Theseus' ship is the 'same' or is 'not the same' as the original one or whether a pile of rice is a 'heap' or is 'not-a-heap'. Yet, because of the particular logic that Standard Western Philosophy uses, it becomes a problem for them.

Another thing about Standard Western Philosophy is that they talk a lot about 'truth'. They say 'This is true', 'That is true', 'That is not true', or 'That is false'. But they don't have a well-defined theory of what is 'true' or 'false'. There's no definitive process for defining or deciding what is 'true' or 'false', and all one is left with is an opinion. My opinion is that it is true; your opinion is that it is false, so what? There is no relevance or significance to either conclusion.

If one wants to include truth in philosophy, one needs an explicit axiomatic system, in the way that mathematics is an explicit axiomatic system. Then in such a system, it can be proven, given certain axioms and rules of inference, that three plus two is five; and then we might say that this is 'true' within that axiomatic system. And because it is all so explicit and obvious, we all accept that '3+2=5' is 'true', within that axiomatic system. (It would not be true if one were to use different symbols or different rules of inference.) So one can label the statement '3+2=5' as being 'true' within the system of mathematics.

The thing about truth is that it needs to be provable; however, that is typically not the way it is done in Standard Western Philosophy. If someone wants to claim that something is 'true', they need to be able to prove it. If they are unable to prove it and don't have proof, then one has to consider the possibility that it is not provable. Then if something is not provable, it is possible that it is not true. Therefore, if it has the possibility of not being true, it is naive to claim that it is true. Yet one can find claims of truth throughout Standard Western Philosophy with nothing resembling any sort of proof.

If something has not been proven, it is naive, within philosophy, to claim that it is true. Yet this is what Standard Western philosophy often does; it claims truth where it is unproven; it claims that its opinions are true. I suspect that it does this because it wishes to popularise its writings by claiming that they are certain and cannot be doubted. For that is what truth is: it is a claim of certainty.

However, subjective certainty is best achieved by simply not considering alternative possibilities; in other words by having a blinkered and myopic approach to philosophy. And this is what has happened. Many of the proponents of Standard Western Philosophy have meekly followed others along the same path, without considering alternatives. As a result, they have found themselves in a blind canyon with walls on each side and a big wall in front so that they can't go any further. There is no way forward except to retrace their steps back to a better starting position and start again.

So can anything be salvaged from Standard Western Philosophy? Well, there are a lot of good ideas, gems if you like, buried within it somewhere within the thousands and thousands of books that have been written. Certainly, there are some very good ideas, and the opinions are often interesting and even sometimes useful, particularly in politics and sociology. People's opinions are important, but they are not philosophy. They are not objective. And they are not true. So its claims of truth are naive.

So apart from the opinions and the few gems that are buried deep within it, Standard Western Philosophy is probably best ignored. There's not a lot that can be done with it.

So instead, we need to start afresh and see if we can find a new philosophical paradigm that is an improvement on the old.

# Chapter 4
# What Makes for a Good
# Philosophical Paradigm?

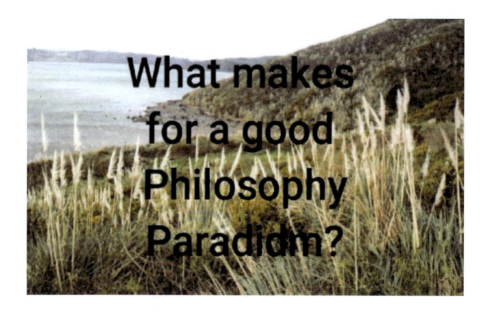

*We have explored how philosophy is a paradigm and that SWP is naive, so now we explore possible criteria for what one might want for a good philosophy paradigm.*

In this chapter, I want to discuss: 'what are the criteria for a good philosophy?' or more specifically for 'a good philosophical paradigm'. This is not so much philosophy itself, it is more meta-philosophy, where one is looking at the whole of philosophy. It is at a level above philosophy, but nevertheless, it is a part of philosophy as well.

So what are the criteria for a good philosophical paradigm? As an introduction to that, there are a couple of similitudes that I would like to look at very briefly. The first is that of science as a paradigm, as presented by Thomas

Kuhn. It is a good idea description of science that it is a collection of ideas that have assumptions and logical processes from which one can reach conclusions which are accurate representations of the world.

Kuhn suggested five criteria for what he considered to be good scientific theory. They were accuracy, self-consistency, explanatory (i.e. explaining more than what the original idea was designed to explain), simplicity and that it should make predictions. These criteria were for a scientific paradigm and one would expect the criteria for a philosophical paradigm to be somewhat similar yet also different.

So the ones I'm suggesting are slightly different from those of Kuhn. I will be including three of his: accuracy, self-consistency and simplicity. The explanatory one and the making predictions one are incorporated to some degree in the other criteria that I will be suggesting.

The second similitude I want to use as an analogy for identifying criteria for a philosophical paradigm is that of the ideas in one's own head. Philosophy is closely linked to the ideas in one's head, for philosophy is done in one's head and the ideas in a person's head that are communicated constitute what is philosophy. So what are the criteria that one might want for the ideas in one's own head? Obviously, self-consistency is one of them; one doesn't want to have discontinuities in one's knowledge.

Also, one doesn't want to create cognitive dissonance where one idea suggests one thing and a different idea in the same domain suggests a contrary thing. One also wants a harmonious, self-consistent whole for the ideas in one's head. So self-consistency might be an important criterion that one would also want for a philosophical paradigm. The other one, of course, is accuracy. The ideas in one's head need to be an accurate representation of the world so that one can interact effectively with the world.

That said, philosophy is different from both of these. It's far more wide-ranging than science, and it has to be much more explicit and more logical than the ideas in one's own head.

The six criteria that I suggest are essential for a good philosophy are:

1.  **Self-consistency**: Clearly, it is important for the ideas in philosophy to be consistent with each other, for otherwise there is chaos. Within a paradigm, one wants all the ideas to be consistent with all the other ideas in that paradigm; and to do so without glitches, schisms and non-

sequiturs. For if there are inconsistencies, it would indicate that there is something wrong with that paradigm, and it needs improvement.

2. **Comprehensiveness.** The requirement for comprehensiveness applies specifically to philosophy because philosophy is a discipline that takes into account all the knowledge of all the other disciplines of science and arts; philosophy ties them all together. So it needs to be comprehensive and incorporate everything about the world. That is what philosophy is all about. If there are gaps in the philosophical paradigm, this may well be because the philosophy within that paradigm is incapable of describing aspects of knowledge within its framework, and this would indicate a limitation on the effectiveness of the philosophy.

3. **Accuracy.** It is important for a philosophy to describe the world accurately. If it doesn't, it would indicate that the philosophical paradigm is relating more to an abstract world or perhaps a fantasy world than the real world. It needs to accurately represent the facts of the world.

4. **Logic.** This is important because logic is the process by which inferences are made, and the ideas within the paradigm need to be logically linked so that one idea can be linked logically with another one. One wants simple logical processes that lead from one idea to another with no jumps in logic or hand-waving arguments.

5. **Explicitness.** A good philosophy needs to be explicit in its foundations and processes of logical inference. For without that, it may be inferred that its arguments are no more than 'hand-waving' and its conclusions unjustified. It also needs to be explicit about how its ideas fit into the facts of reality, for without that it could be inferred that the ideas only relate to a fantasy world.

6. **Simplicity.** To some degree, simplicity is not essential, but nevertheless, one does prefer simplicity to complexity. A good philosophical paradigm needs to be simple so that it shows clarity of ideas. Also, communication is an essential part of the practice of philosophy and simple ideas and simple language are far more conducive to effective communication than complicated and convoluted language. But that said, some ideas are inherently complex, but nevertheless, they need to be presented in as simple a form as possible.

Those are my suggestions for the criteria for a good philosophical paradigm: Self-consistency, Comprehensiveness, Accuracy, Logic, Explicitness and Simplicity. I have put them in this order so that the first letters spell the acronym SCALES; a useful way to remember them.

# Chapter 5
# How Does Standard Western Philosophy Stack Up as a Philosophy Paradigm?

*We now turn to the prevailing and traditional Western philosophy to evaluate its efficacy.*

In the previous chapter, we discussed 6 criteria for a good philosophy and gave them the acronym SCALES for Self-consistency, Comprehensiveness, Accuracy, Logic, Explicitness and Simplicity.

In this chapter, we will be using these criteria to make an estimate of the efficacy of Standard Western Philosophy (SWP) as a philosophical paradigm. The method used for this is certainly subjective but the end result is interesting.

What do I mean by standard Western philosophy? As mentioned in a previous chapter, I mean everything that is in the canon of modern Western philosophy, including all of what might be found in any university library in the philosophy section.

Standard Western Philosophy is a collection of ideas on philosophy with many different facets and assertions, yet they all share a common set of core ideas. Standard Western Philosophy sets the benchmark for philosophy. It can trace its roots to the start of philosophical investigations in ancient Greece. It focuses heavily on language with its propositions, arguments and statements; it considers that truth is a property of statements and that objective truth can be encapsulated within true statements. It also relies heavily on the history and tradition of philosophy.

So now we look at the SCALES criteria and give a score out of ten to SWP for each category.

### 1. Self-consistency

The criteria of self-consistency look at whether the ideas within the paradigm are consistent with each other. While Standard Western Philosophy does try to be self-consistent, there are two problems of self-consistency that come to mind. First, the paradoxes of language such as 'the ship of Theseus' and 'the heap' are discussed in Chapter 3. Standard Western Philosophy considers these to be problems of philosophy, but of course, they are only problems of the Standard Western Philosophy paradigm.

The second and more significant one is that while it has been identified in Standard Western Philosophy that there is a distinction between the noumena, the things that supposedly actually exist and the phenomena which are the perception of those things and that the divide between the two cannot be crossed, i.e. all we actually know about the physical world are phenomena. Nevertheless, Standard Western Philosophy still holds that truths about the world are identifiable and further that these truths can be expressed in statements. This is a major inconsistency. Nevertheless, I will give Standard Western Philosophy a score of 5 out of 10 for self-consistency.

### 2. Comprehensiveness

Philosophy is about everything in the world and an effective philosophical paradigm needs to cover all aspects of the world; hence comprehensiveness is important for a philosophical paradigm. Standard Western Philosophy does cover many aspects of the world, but there are a few glaring omissions.

1. In its ethics, it focuses solely on what is best for the community and other people. It has very little to say about what is best for the individual.
2. It says nothing about the very human activities of sleep, consciousness or laughter.
3. Despite using the word 'truth' a lot, it has no definitive theory of what truth is, how it is used nor how it can be determined what is to be labelled as 'truth' and what is not.
4. Despite being focused heavily on words and language, it has no theory for how words are logically linked to the real world. Instead, it relies on defining words in terms of other words, but this is ultimately circular. It lacks an effective theory for how words are linked to the world. And this is problematic, for without such a theory and with a focus on language, there is no process by which meaningful words can be distinguished from non-meaningful or fanciful words that belong more to the realm of fantasy than philosophy.

Overall, I can score Standard Western Philosophy 5 out of 10 for comprehensiveness.

## 3. Accuracy

Accuracy is important to any philosophy in that it is an indication of how well that theory fits the facts. If this connection is not well established then it may be that the philosophy only has relevance to a fantasy or non-real world and not to the actual real world. It is not sufficient to merely take normative facts of the world and claim that they are 'true'. There needs to be powerful explanative theories that describe many and possibly diverse facts of the world. Standard Western Philosophy seems to lack these powerful theories. Its theory that every statement is either true or false might seem to be reasonable, but if this is an accurate theory then one would expect there to be a list of statements that were 'true' and another list of statements that were 'false'; however, these seem to be missing from the canon of Standard Western Philosophy, presumably because such a list cannot be formed.

Nevertheless, I will give standard philosophy a score of 5 out of 10 for accuracy.

## 4.  Logic

Standard Western philosophy certainly tries to be rigorous and logical, but because it focuses so much on language and words it is not really rigorous nor even logical. Its problem stems from failing to distinguish between a word as a string of alphanumeric symbols, words in a dictionary, ideas in one's head and something that exists in the real world. For example, in its logic, it is not clear whether the word 'tree' is to be treated as a string of alphanumeric symbols 't', 'r', 'e', 'e' or as a word in a dictionary that can be linked to other words such as 'shrub' or 'bush' within the dictionary or as the idea of a tree in one's head or as the possibility of a real tree existing somewhere in reality. Standard Western Philosophy does not distinguish between these possibilities; instead what it does is bundle all these different interpretations of 'tree' together and use them in a logic that is little more than hand-waving. I call it hand-waving as it does not use any explicit or logical process by which words can be manipulated or processed.

So overall, I can only give standard Western philosophy a score of 3 out of 10 for logic.

## 5.  Explicitness

Philosophy needs to be explicit with regard to its foundations and its processes of inference; otherwise, it is indistinguishable from opinion. By 'opinion', I mean the conclusions reached by means of a process that is hidden from everyone else. Hence, opinions are entirely subjective and specific only to the person presenting the opinion. Others might agree with it if they share similar knowledge and thought processes, but even so, it remains a subjective opinion. Standard Western Philosophy is not at all explicit as to its foundation nor its processes of inference.

It has its claims of logic, but as already discussed, this logic is not particularly rigorous, and even so, that logic is not used very much in the actual inferential processes within the theses of Standard Western Philosophy. As such, much of Standard Western Philosophy can be classified as opinion. It may be considered a thoughtful opinion but nevertheless remains a subjective opinion. And this also applies to its claims of 'truth'; as previously mentioned Standard Western Philosophy has no explicit and logical theory of truth; the best it can do is to claim that a statement is 'true' if it corresponds to the facts of reality, but it has no theory for the logic of 'corresponds' nor any process by which it can be determined whether a statement actually 'corresponds' to the facts of reality or not, that is anything more than a hand-waving process. And so its claims of truth are no more than subjective opinions.

So I can only give Standard Western Philosophy a score of 2 out of 10 for explicitness.

## 6. Simplicity

Simplicity is important as it indicates clarity of thought and clarity of ideas. Standard Western Philosophy is neither simple in its ideas nor in its communication of those ideas. The lack of clarity in its writings is undoubtedly linked to the lack of clarity of its ideas.

So overall I can only give Standard Western Philosophy a score of 1 out of 10 for simplicity.

So now totalling up the scores and taking a simple average, one arrives at an overall score of 3.5 out of 10 for the efficacy of Standard Western Philosophy as a philosophical paradigm.

While this score is entirely a subjective opinion, it is one that may be well-shared by others. In any case, it would seem that there is room for considerable improvement. Whether this improvement can be achieved within the paradigm and using the precepts of Standard Western Philosophy or whether a paradigm shift is required is a moot point.

*This provides a benchmark for a philosophical paradigm; one that we shall attempt to improve upon during the course of our journey.*

# Chapter 6
# Preparation for a Philosophical Journey

*We are now ready to move on from the meta-philosophy and can turn to the*
*philosophy of the Pattern Paradigm itself.*

When I began my research into philosophy, the aim was to explore the roots of philosophy to the deepest level. The result was the creation of a framework for the logic of thinking that accurately describes the world.

For the description of the Pattern Paradigm in this book, we shall be starting at the deepest level and then progressing upwards and outwards.

The aim of the journey is to construct an overall view of the world from just a few basic assumptions and an explicit logical process. If this can be achieved, we will have arrived at a philosophy that is comprehensive, simple, self-consistent and an accurate view of the world. The benefit of this is that one will have a better understanding of the world and a better model of the world, which should enable one to make better decisions regarding one's life.

There is no requirement for any particular philosophical paradigm to fit with any other philosophical paradigm. So in this book, I make no attempt to correlate the ideas of TPP with any other philosophy. In fact, in places, I expose the flaws of some of the ideas in other philosophies, especially SWP; just in case readers might think that those ideas are indubitable and must necessarily be a part of any philosophical paradigm.

Nevertheless, the writings of philosophers past have undoubtedly been influential in the creation of this philosophy, even if it was only an indication of what to avoid.

It is perhaps the writings of the philosopher David Hume with which there is most agreement with TPP. However, Hume's writings typically highlighted what was not possible in rational thought rather than what was possible; such as uncertainty of inferences, the myth of causality, that you cannot get a 'should' from an 'is', and his dismissal of any philosophical writing that does not fit with either facts of the world or what he called 'relations of ideas'.

So to some degree, I consider TPP to be a continuation of Hume's treatises, but into a positive realm using, in particular, the concepts of evolution and computation, both of which were unheard of at the time of Hume.

(In contrast, much of SWP follows from the works of Kant who came after Hume. I have no doubt that Hume would have refuted Kant's claims if he had had the chance.)

Philosophy is a paradigm and if it is to be a good paradigm it must be founded on explicit assumptions. While it may be expedient for the assumptions to be reasonable within the context of common knowledge, it is not a necessary requirement; the test of a good philosophical paradigm is that the theorems that emanate from those assumptions provide an accurate description of the world and lead to a new and better understanding of the world.

So what are the foundational assumptions of TPP?

The first assumption is with regard to the concept of evolution. We will be making the assumption that life, including human life, evolved on Earth through the process of evolution. There is no need for us to go into the details of DNA or genotypes or phenotypes or exactly how it all works. It is sufficient for us to know that the details of the process are available should we want or need to explore them further. The main point of taking evolution with us as an assumption is that it provides an excellent theory for the origins and processes of life. It explains it as a physical and natural process; one that does not require some sort of spontaneous creation or intrinsic mystery.

The second assumption we shall make is that the brain of an animal can be modelled by a logical processor. All animals and humans have some sort of brain or logical processor that makes decisions regarding how the animal reacts to particular situations. So in order to understand human (and animal) life, we need to assume the existence of a logical processor as one of the original essential organs of the animal's body. We can further assume, given that we have already made the assumption of evolution, that this logical processor or brain evolved in much the same way as the other organs of an animal's body evolved, such as the eye, heart and liver.

In the same way that we don't need to know the details of how evolution works, we don't need to know the details of how the brain evolved. Also, being philosophy, we don't need to know the physical or hardware characteristics of the brain or logical processor. All we need to know is that it is a logical processor and that it exists as a core organ of the animal's, and especially the human's, body.

What do I mean by a logical processor? Perhaps the best analogy is that of a small computer. All it can do is follow the rules to create inferences. Also, it has some form of data input and data output and can store and retrieve data, but that is all. And 'what rules does it follow?' one might ask. Well, so far there are no rules. What rules our logical processor follows will have to be created through a process of evolution.

And what is logic? Logic is a process in which symbols or bits of data are manipulated according to specific rules to generate an output.

Note: While the brain itself is a physical entity and is subject to the 'laws of physics', we can interpret the processes of the brain in the form of a logical model. It is similar to the distinction between the hardware and software of a computer. The hardware is the physical entity of the computer and is subject to the 'laws of physics' whereas its software constitutes a model of its logical processes.

The third thing we shall take on our journey, but which is not really an assumption, is a compass. The compass will point us in the direction in which we want to go, which is in the direction of normative human experience. Without such a compass and a direction to go in, we would have to explore every logical possibility and might go around in circles or possibly end up with a philosophy more suited to a giraffe or a crocodile. With a compass, we can proceed in one direction towards our goal: a description of the world as we experience it.

So, for our journey, this is all we need to take. We can leave behind all the tenets and claims of truth of other philosophies, for they will only be an encumbrance.

# Chapter 7
# The Deepest Depths of Philosophy

*We begin the next stage of our journey by diving into the depths of a place and time where there is only matter and look at how the first glimmer of mind can appear.*

In the previous chapter, we discussed the preparation for our philosophical journey and how we would only take with us the concept of evolution, a logical processor and a compass. In this chapter, I want to go to the very depths of philosophy and suggest how a division between the material and the immaterial might be manifest.

So let's start with some material, I will be using some wooden blocks to illustrate what I am suggesting. Here are some wooden bricks:

They are matter, purely matter, just blocks of wood.
But suppose I arrange them in a particular way…

In this particular form, the blocks of wood become something more than just matter; matter has become symbolic. These are symbols that we recognise, and these symbols can have significance.

I could change it just a little bit and move just one block…

Then the whole significance of the symbols changes.
Or I can arrange the blocks in this way…

Then again the significance of the symbols represented by the pieces of wood changes.

For all these arrangements, from one perspective they are just blocks of wood, yet from different processing of the data, the arrangement of the blocks of wood can take on symbolic significance.

Symbols are just symbols, but if they are interpreted in a particular way through a logical processor they can take on a significance that transcends the pure substance of the blocks.

The separation of the immaterial from the material comes through an arrangement of material, and this arrangement can be symbolic and significant.

People are both material and immaterial. We all have a mind and awareness that is unique to us What I am suggesting is that it is the arrangement of the material of which we are composed that allows for our immaterial minds.

But where does this significance come from, and how is it achieved? How can it be created out of nothing?

Where can we start to explore the development of symbols and their significance? I suggest we begin with the concept of evolution and a logical processor as mentioned at the start of this chapter.

Let us go to a time of evolution at the very start of animal life; it is a world full of plant life. There we will look at a primeval animal and how it might interact with the world. We will allow this animal to have sensory organs such as vision or perhaps smell, and perhaps some internal senses as well so as to evaluate its overall well-being, including such things as the fullness of its stomach. It also has motor outputs that enable it to move its body and perhaps have a biting movement with its mouth. It also has a proto-brain that controls its motor outputs in response to its sensory data.

While this proto-brain is a physical entity in the same way that a heart or liver are physical entities; its operation can be modelled using a set of rules that determine how it operates.

It is important to note that at this stage of development, the logical processor has no concepts of anything; it has no concepts of its sensory data nor its motor outputs; it only has rules that determine how it processes the sense-data and how it operates its motor outputs.

The question now is: What sort of rules could it have in the logic of its proto-brain that would enable it to function as a viable animal? Clearly, these rules will be developed through trial and error and a process of evolution; some will work effectively, and the animal thrives, whereas other rules will not work, and the animal and its genes will not survive.

So now we will use our compass to point in the direction of the sort of rules that would enable the animal to flourish (this enables us to take a shortcut through the trials and errors of evolution). So what might these rules be?

At the most elementary level, the animal can ignore the sense-data and simply use its motor outputs to alternately move forward and bite, move forward and bite. This could be an effective strategy if it is immersed in a field of edible plants. But of course, that will not always be the case.

At a slightly higher level, the animal can take a portion of the data from its senses and then depending on the rules it is working with it can interact with the world.

We can illustrate this using the wooden blocks. Suppose the animal encounters some data, it could be visual or olfactory, and it can store the data symbolically as represented by this square shape:

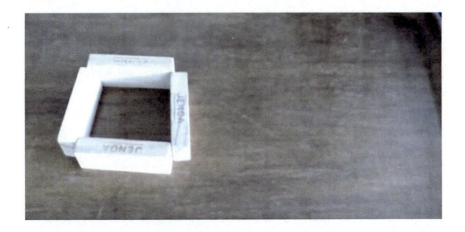

Suppose the rules of the logical processor are along the lines of:

'if the data is unrecognised move forward and bite'. Perhaps the animal does not recognise this shape and so moves forward and bites. Then the associated information from the stomach, which we can represent with a stone, can be stored alongside the original data.

So that is what the animal does, and we can represent it like this:

So what we have here is one bit of data (the square) associated with a different bit of data (the stone).

Suppose then it encounters a different set of data: (represented by the triangle)

It does not recognise the shape and so again, it moves forward and bites. This time the signal from its stomach is different and can be represented by the shell. So it stores that too within its logical processor.

And then it encounters another bit of data which is this:

It recognises it, and it is associated with the stone.

Suppose that among its rules it is the rule: 'if a piece of data is associated with a stone then move forward and bite, while if it is associated with a shell then avoid it and go elsewhere'. So our animal encounters the above bit of data and associates it with a stone. So it moves forward and bites. It continues to do this for the rest of its life, which is unfortunately rather short, and it dies. It does not survive to pass on its genes.

But it has a sibling; with very similar logical rules, except that the rules for the sibling are reversed such that 'if a piece of data is associated with a shell then move forward and bite while if it is associated with a stone, then avoid it and go elsewhere'.

So then the sibling comes along, and it sees a bit of data like this:

It associates it with the stone:

Following its rules, it avoids it; then it comes across a bit of data like this.

It associates this bit of data with the shell and following its rules, it moves forward, and bites. Happily, this organism survives and reproduces and its genes pass on.

As observers of these events, we can infer that the stone which represents data from its stomach is an indication that its stomach is 'not happy' whereas the shell represents data that the stomach 'is happy'. We can further infer that the sense-data represented by the triangle comes from something that is nutritious for the proto-animal and that the square represents data from something that is not good to eat.

What I am showing here is how a primitive animal can use its logical processor to interact with the world to benefit itself in an entirely mechanical way. And also to show how evolution can impact the logical rules which it follows.

The primitive proto-animal has no idea of what it is doing, it is entirely inanimate. It is interacting with its environment in an entirely mechanical way. It has no conception of anything; neither itself nor the world. No matter how complex or refined this system, of storing data and reacting to it, becomes, the logical processor can never be more than an inanimate machine.

Much the same goes for modern computers and artificial intelligence; they are entirely inanimate; they have no concept of themselves or the world or anything.

Nevertheless, symbolism combined with rules is the start of the development of something more than just matter and can lead to the development of a non-mechanical mind. But how is this possible?

We know that it is possible because we humans have achieved that state. We have concepts of the world; we have an understanding of the world. So how is it possible that a proto-animal such as we have been discussing could evolve into an animal that has awareness of itself and of its environment in the way that we humans do? This will be discussed in the next part of our journey.

# Chapter 8
## Patterns, Time and Space

*Our journey now takes us to perhaps the most significant part of our journey, in which we explore the logical processes by which a model of the world can be created ex nihilo; how a concept can be created in a place where there were no concepts before.*

In the previous chapter, we looked at how a logical processor that has links to sense-data and also to motor outputs, can interact with its environment in order to benefit itself. We looked at a number of examples of how this would work. This is the very beginning of how a logical processor can interact with the world, but it is far from the sort of way that we humans interact with the world. There is a significant difference between a simple logical processor interacting with the world in an entirely mechanical way, and the way that we humans interact with the world, for we humans have a model of the world and an understanding of how different concepts are related. This is totally different from how computers operate as they do not have a model of the world. So how is it possible for a logical processor to create a model of the world? What might be the logical processes that could allow this to happen?

Let us return to the proto-animal with the proto-brain; it has senses, motor outputs and a logical processor. But this time, rather than just looking at the most primitive means of interacting with the world, we will look at how it can create concepts and the beginning of a model of the world.

Here we are using the compass that we brought with us on our journey. We know that proto-animals began with no concepts of anything, and we know that animals have evolved to humans who have lots of concepts of lots of things; so we know that somehow this transition was effected over the many millions of years of evolution. The question is: How? What logical process can effect this transition?

I suggest that the only way this can be achieved is through a process of pattern identification. No other logical process for analysing data, whether it be adding or subtracting elements of the data can lead to anything remotely resembling a concept.

However, pattern identification is not a simple logical process. It requires rules that can loop around. It is not a simple linear process in which one simply processes the data and out pops the best pattern.

Instead, the logical process of identifying a pattern requires a starting template in the form of a possible pattern which can then be tested against the data to see if it is indeed the best pattern. The input template could be a segment of the data, or it could be an entirely random set of symbols. Then one can test it to see whether it fits the data or not. If it fits one can move on while if it doesn't one can go back and find a different template and try that.

So let's look at a few examples:

Take this sequence of dollar signs:

$$$$$$$$$

Now I am sure one will quickly recognise that the unit pattern is a dollar sign.

| Data sequence | Pattern Unit | Application |
|---|---|---|
| $$$$$$$$$ | $ | Simple repetition |

Then in order to recreate the data, one can just repeat that dollar sign. So the single dollar sign is the pattern for that particular sequence of dollar signs.

$$ $$ $$ $$ $$ $$

Or you might have this sequence of two dollar signs and a gap, another two dollar signs and a gap. The pattern unit is obviously two dollar signs.

| Data sequence | Pattern Unit | Application |
|---|---|---|
| $$ $$ $$ $$ $$ $$ | $$ | Simple repetition |

Or one might get slightly different ones like '$# $# $# $# $# $#', and then the unit pattern for that is '$#'.

| Data sequence | Pattern Unit | Application |
|---|---|---|
| $# $# $# $# $# $# | $# | Simple repetition |

Or one might get the sequence: '$# $# $% $# $# $#' which is the same as the previous example but has one '#' symbol replaced by a '%' symbol.

| Data sequence | Pattern Unit | Application |
|---|---|---|
| $# $# $% $# $# $# | $# | Simple repetition |

Again the pattern unit is $#, despite it not being entirely accurate. For one could make the assumption that the percentage sign is a spurious bit of data. Or perhaps it is real, but one would need more data in order to identify that that percentage data point was valid and that one wants to accommodate it in one's pattern. To some degree, there is a balance between having an efficient pattern that is very simple and adequately accurate and one that is more accurate but which is not so simple.

Then one might get the sequence: '$#@% $#@% $#@% $#@%' and so on. For this, the pattern would be $#@% repeated as a sequence.

| Data sequence | Pattern Unit | Application |
|---|---|---|
| $#@% $#@% $#@% $#@% | $#@% | Simple repetition |

What one is doing in finding a pattern is compressing the data. One is taking a long string of data and compressing it so that the pattern unit is a compressed form of the string of data and can be used to recreate the original data. While this pattern-identifying process is not entirely linear, it is nevertheless entirely logical because one can write its rules as a simple algorithm. Having an algorithm is very important for demonstrating and describing a logical process. So one can have a simple algorithm which describes the pattern identification process:

**Algorithm for pattern identification.**

1. Assemble the data.
2. Input a template (e.g. a sample of the data)
3. Test the template; Does it fit?
4. If it doesn't fit return to step 2.
5. Else continue
6. Store the template together with a label for the data.

People are very adept at finding patterns. (In contrast, a lot of people find mathematics and the manipulation of mathematical symbols to be very tricky.) But when it comes to finding a pattern for data, like some of the ones I have just shown, people find it very easy. So that is an indication that we are on the right track in our journey for identifying the logical processes for creating a model of the world.

To show how fundamental this is I would like to show another couple of examples. Take this example where one has a sequence of data:

$ $$ $$$ $$$$ $$$$$ $$$$$$ etc.

What is the pattern there? It is not hard to identify: it is a dollar and then the next one in the sequence is two dollars the next one is three dollars the next one is four dollars and so on.

| Data sequence | Pattern Unit | Application |
|---|---|---|
| $ $$ $$$ $$$$ $$$$$ $$$$$$ | $ | Add a unit for each repetition |

So going back to the physical animal, what sort of sense-data might produce a sequence like this? I suggest that if the animal is moving towards the source of the sense-data (it could be visual, or it could be sound, or it could be smell); as the animal approaches the source of the data, the signal gets stronger. In this way, it can identify the beginnings of space; a spatial recognition as it moves in a particular way towards the source of sense-data (not that the animal, at this stage in the creation of its model of the world, is aware that it is moving), it gets a first impression of space.

Another example, suppose one has the sense-data of the form: '####@@@@####@@@@####' and so on. Obviously, we can identify what the pattern is here; it is '###@@@@'.

| Data sequence | Pattern Unit | Application |
|---|---|---|
| ####@@@@####@@@@#### | ####@@@@ | Simple repetition |

Going back to our organism again, this could possibly represent the sequence of day and night; it is light for a certain time, and then it is dark for a certain time, light for a certain time, dark for a certain time and so on. In this way, it gets the first impression of time.

So using this pattern identification process, we have looked at the very roots of the identification of time and space. It is interesting to note that Standard Western Philosophy merely labels time and space as 'a priori' and just leaves it at that, without any depth nor understanding. In contrast, we have looked beneath that to the basic logical processes of identifying what is time and what is space.

This process of pattern identification and data compression enables the creation of a very elementary model of the world. It enables the primeval animal to begin to make sense of the data it receives in something more than a merely mechanical way.

I suggest that there is no other purely logical process that is capable of processing sense-data which has the possibility of creating concepts from a situation where there were no concepts before.

It may seem to be quite a leap of logical rules from the simple reaction to sense-data in a purely mechanical way described in the previous chapter to one where one has a considerably more complex algorithm for identifying patterns. Yet it is a leap that the evolution of the brain clearly made. Presumably, it made the leap in little steps in much the same way as our eyes developed in little steps.

I further suggest that this pattern-identifying process is fundamental to thinking and hence is fundamental to philosophy.

It may be of interest to note that this theory of pattern identification is itself a consequence of the process of pattern identification given the specific data mentioned at the beginning of this chapter. In other words, this theory of pattern identification is the best pattern to fit the relevant data.

But in order to construct a full model of the world, we need something more than just creating simple patterns from simple sense-data; that is not going to be enough; we need something more. This will be discussed in the next chapter.

# Chapter 9
# Pyramids, Patterns and Why We Sleep

*Our journey continues to the realm of creating a comprehensive model of the world.*

At the start of our journey, we talked about a very primitive logical processor as might have been the case at the very start of animal evolution.

In the previous chapter: 'Patterns Time and Space', we discussed how the logical processes of pattern identification could be used to begin to make sense of raw sense-data. It was also noted that the process of pattern identification is the only logical process by which raw sense-data can be interpreted without any form of preconception of what the raw sense-data might comprise. The algorithm for this logical process is something like:

1. Assemble the data.
2. Input a template.
3. Test the template—does it fit?

4.  If it fits, continue; Otherwise return to step 2
5.  Store the template together with a label for the data.

While this process is able to simplify and begin to make sense of the world from the raw sense-data, something more is required to create a comprehensive model of the world such as what we humans experience. So what is it? What we could try is, instead of using raw data as input to the pattern-identifying process we could use the already identified patterns as input to the pattern-identified process and hence create a higher-level pattern.

Let us look at some examples of the sort of patterns that might be created from sense-data. For these examples, I will be using simple arithmetic to model the examples.

| Data | Pattern | Label |
|------|---------|-------|
| 1 2 3 4 5 | n | A |

In these examples 'Data' represents the sense-data, 'Pattern' represents the pattern that best fits the data, 'Label' is just a label to identify that particular pattern, and 'n' represents the counting numbers and denotes the position of a data element in the sequence.

The justification for the representation of data as strings of numbers is that computers have shown that a variety of types of data such as pictures and sounds can be stored as strings of numbers; they just need specific rules and special equipment to convert these numbers back into pictures or music.

So suppose the data took the form of 1, 2, 3, 4, 5 and we used the algorithm at the start of this chapter to find a pattern, then the pattern would be 'n' where 'n' denotes the position of the different data elements, and then we might label that pattern as A.

Then suppose that we had some more data which took the form 2 4 6 8 and 10. Fairly obviously the pattern would be 2n, and we can label that as B. And so on till we get the table below. Note that the identifying pattern is a compressed form of the data and that by using the pattern we can recreate the data.

| Data | Pattern | Label | Recreated Data |
|------|---------|-------|----------------|
| 1 2 3 4 5 | n | A | 1 2 3 4 5 |
| 2 4 6 8 10 | 2n | B | 2 4 6 8 10 |
| 3 6 9 12 15 | 3n | C | 3 6 9 12 15 |
| 4 8 12 16 20 | 4n | D | 4 8 12 16 20 |

So now we have some patterns that fit the raw data; where do we go from here? What if now instead of using the raw sense-data as the input to the pattern-identifying process we used the identified patterns as input? Then we would have as our input data n, 2n, 3n and 4n.

If we now fed these patterns into the pattern-identifying algorithm as data, then the pattern would be m times n, where m represents the position in the input sequence of the data. We could label that ZZ.

| Data | Pattern | Label | Recreated Data |
|------|---------|-------|----------------|
| n 2n 3n 4n | m X n | ZZ | n 2n 3n 4n |

What we have arrived at is a pattern of patterns.

This pattern has the capability of recreating the original level 0 data:

| Raw Data | Level 1 Pattern | Level 2 Pattern | | Recreated Data |
|----------|-----------------|-----------------|---|----------------|
| 1 2 3 4 5 | n | [ | ] | 1 2 3 4 5...... |
| 2 4 6 8 10 | 2n | [ | ] | 2 4 6 8 10... |
| 3 6 9 12 15 | 3n | [ m X n ] | | 3 6 9 12 15... |
| 4 8 12 16 20 | 4n | [ | ] | 4 8 12 16 20.... |
| 5 10 15 20 25 | 5n | [ | ] | 5 10 15 20 25... |

This process of putting the identified patterns back into the pattern-identifying process as input data does not have to stop at level 2.

When a sufficient number of patterns of patterns have been identified at level two, these can be assembled and subsequently used as input to the pattern-identifying algorithm to generate a level 3 pattern.

This process of taking the output of a logical process and reinserting it as input for the same logical process is called 'recursion'. Since pattern identification is necessarily the compression of the data, the quantity of patterns at each level will be smaller than the level below it. Then if we draw a schematic diagram for these levels of patterns we arrive at something that has the shape of a step pyramid where each higher level is smaller than the level below it. So then one has raw sense-data at the bottom, then above that there are the level 1 patterns, above that the level 2 patterns and so on for however far one wants to go. In this way, we can create a model of the world based on raw sense-data.

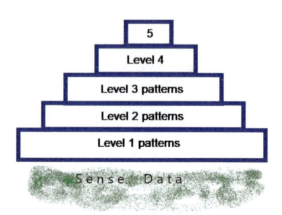

We saw in the previous chapter how patterns created from sense-data could lead to the beginnings of concepts of time and space. Other patterns from sense-data could similarly be associated with concepts for various foods, objects, plants, animals and so on.

So let us look at another example of how this might work. For this example, I will only be using the labels of the patterns to designate the patterns as the actual details of the patterns themselves would be highly complex. Nevertheless, it is actually the details of the patterns which are used in the pattern-identifying process, and these labels are just labels for the underlying patterns.

Suppose at level 1, one has the labels for the patterns of 'leaf', 'branch', 'fruit' and 'trunk':

Then these patterns might be combined into a higher-level pattern which is then given the label 'tree'.

This level 2 pattern of 'tree' could be combined with other level 2 patterns, created in a similar manner, such as 'bush', 'flower' and 'vine'.

And then together with a tree, these might be combined into a pattern found which is then given the label 'forest'.

And that would be a level 3 pattern. Then this level 3 pattern labelled 'forest' can be combined with other level 3 patterns which might be 'grassland', 'river' and 'hill'.

Then they might be combined into a pattern which is given the label 'land'.

This would be a level 4 pattern and the level 4 pattern labelled as 'land' could be combined with other patterns for things such as 'town' or 'sea'

In this way, one arrives at a pyramid of patterns. And this pyramid of patterns constitutes one's beliefs or knowledge about the world. It constitutes a model of the world.

This line of reasoning for the creation of a model of the world from pattern identification of sense-data, recursion and the creation of a pyramid of patterns may be somewhat simplistic. However, it shows how a model of the world can be created from fundamental principles.

Only through the process of pattern identification, can a model of the world be created.

The actual process of pattern identification through all levels is a complex one: data has to be assembled, possible templates tested then the accuracy of the resulting patterns evaluated before a final pattern is selected.

It is a long and time-consuming process and so for higher patterns to be found, when using the recursion process, this would be best done when the logical processor or brain is not busy doing anything else such as evaluating raw data from its senses searching for food, evading predators and so on. So this would best be achieved when the animal has found a place of safety and closed off its senses so that its logical processor or brain can focus on searching for higher-level patterns; in other words when the animal is asleep.

This provides an explanation for why we need sleep. It is an essential requirement for our brains to create a comprehensive model of the world, and it is also an explanation for why babies need so much sleep as their brains work overtime in searching for patterns that will enable them to make sense of the world in which they find themselves. It should be noted that this explanation for sleep is emergent from the theory we have been discussing; from the assumptions and logic already described in this journey. The fact that it is emergent and that it fits well with our experience is further evidence that we are on the right track in this journey.

Finally in this chapter, I would like to discuss very briefly the labels that are used to identify patterns. Patterns that are near the base in the pyramid of patterns have labels that remain hidden from us. So, for example, patterns that we use to interpret light and shade as shadows are hidden from us and yet they enable us to perceive a three-dimensional world from the two-dimensional data we receive from our eyes.

However, for higher-level patterns the labels are equivalent to what we call 'words'; or to put it another way words are labels for patterns. Words like 'run', 'tree', 'elephant' and so on are all labels for patterns that have been created ultimately from sense-data through the pattern identification process.

It is interesting to note that Standard Western Philosophy has no theory for what a word is. Here is a quote from the Stanford Encyclopedia of Philosophy on the internet: "The notions of word and word meaning are problematic to pin down, and this is reflected in the difficulties one encounters in defining the basic terminology of lexical semantics." In other words, they have no idea what a word is. Yet their whole philosophy is based on words and the manipulation of words; all without any viable theory of what a word actually is. But as we have seen, and according to the Pattern Paradigm which I am describing in this book, a word is a label for a pattern.

# Chapter 10
# The Foundations of Reality and Purpose

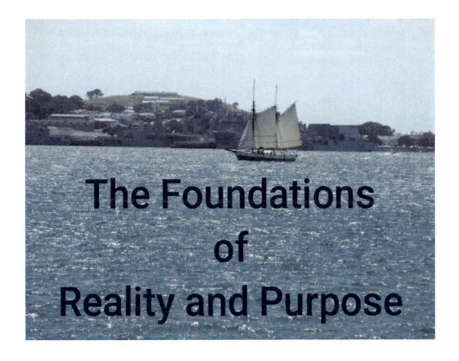

*Our journey continues into the realm of the concept of reality; how our organism with its logical processor can interact with the world and how its purpose enables it to meet its basic requirements.*

In this chapter, I want to take a look at how one's pyramid of patterns that we discussed in the previous chapter can be incorporated into one's life. In order to do this, I will first give a brief recap of how a pyramid of patterns can be created.

In the journey so far, we have looked at how an animal, at the start of the evolution of animals and which has a logical processor, can begin to make sense of the world and create a model of the world. It was realised that the only logical way that this could occur was through a process of pattern identification i.e. examining the sense-data and trying various templates, or possible patterns, that could be used to compress the data and to make sense of it. By 'pattern' I am not talking about the whole picture of what one might call a pattern; I am referring to a 'pattern' as the smallest element that can be used to recreate the data.

Creating a pattern from the data is a logical process, and it actually gives information about the nature of the source behind the sense-data; for once a pattern has been identified, it can be extrapolated, perhaps in time or space, beyond the range of the original data. Also, it should be noted that the best pattern to fit a set of data is one that compresses the data the most i.e. a simpler pattern is to be preferred to a more complex one and also one wants a pattern that is best able to reproduce the data most accurately i.e. it fits the data most accurately and that is what I will be referring to as the most efficient pattern, or perhaps the 'best pattern'.

We also looked at how data from the observation of change of light through day and night, could lead to the pattern that we might today associate with 'time', i.e. the regular cycle of day and night leads to the concept or pattern of 'time'. We also looked at how the observation of the changing apparent size of an object as an animal activates some motor outputs and moves 'towards' or 'away' from a particular object, its visual data will make the object appear bigger or smaller, and in this way, this could lead to a pattern that today we might associate with 'space'.

We further noted in the previous chapter that the pattern generation process can be reapplied to the patterns in a recursive manner so that the patterns that have been created from raw sense-data themselves go through the pattern identification process. (For the patterns themselves consist of data in the same way that data from the senses is data.) This creates a higher-level pattern. This can be repeated later on to create further and higher levels of patterns. It was suggested that the overall shape these levels of patterns would present would be like a pyramid. This pyramid would then be representative of one's model of the world. In this way, a comprehensive model of the world can be generated.

In this chapter, I want to talk about how this model of the world can be used in a practical way and how it becomes 'real'. In an earlier chapter, we looked at how the ability to recognise specific sense-data, such as a square shape, could benefit an animal in distinguishing things that might be good to eat from those that are not good to eat. This ability to interact effectively with the world is boosted by having a comprehensive pyramid of patterns and an accurate model of the world. Using its pyramid of patterns, the animal will be better able to find food, find shelter, evade danger and so on.

Not only does the animal have senses, but it also has motor outputs. By motor outputs, I am referring to signals that can be sent from the brain to the animal's muscles to put those in motion such as their arms, legs, mouth or whatever. Clearly, the animal will have to learn, by trial and error, which signals activate which muscles. It will also have to use data from the different parts of its body to create patterns for its arms, legs, wings, mouth etc. in order to create concepts of them and to integrate them with its overall pyramid of patterns.

Once it has achieved this, it can interact with its environment more effectively: finding food, evading predators, finding shelter and locating other members of its species with whom to breed. It is this ability to interact effectively with its environment that reinforces the animal's confidence in the accuracy of its model of the world. In this way, its model of the world, its pyramid of patterns, becomes the reality in which it lives.

The external senses that an animal possesses such as sight, sound, taste and so on are the foundation for the creation of its pyramid of patterns and model of the world. However, the animal also possesses internal senses that provide information about the status of its physical body. These senses are linked to the major organs of the body such as the skin, stomach, heart, liver and so on. Typically, one might consider these signals from the organs as being of pleasure or pain. These internal senses provide the direction and motivation for the animal's interactions with the world. They motivate it to find food, to find shelter, to avoid predators and so on.

The animal's stomach will indicate that it needs sustenance, so the animal will look for food and if its skin indicates that it is cold the animal will seek shelter and so on. It is the fulfilment of the animal's physical needs that provide the purpose and motivation for the life of the animal.

The actual levels of pleasure and pain felt by the animal from its various organs will be set by trial and error within evolution. Some levels of pleasure and pain within a particular animal will be less accentuated than they are for others and so the animal's ability to thrive and reproduce may be less than for others; so the balance between them is set through evolution. But for each individual animal, their goal is to maximise their pleasure and minimise their pain. This provides the motivation and purpose to their life.

It is the combination of external sense-data and internal sense-data together with the decisions that the animal makes and the sending of appropriate signals to its motor outputs that constitutes the animal's reality. Its ability to interact effectively with the world gives it confirmation that the world it lives in is real. This is the world in which the animal operates and hopefully thrives.

In summary: the basic function of the animal consists of taking its external sense-data, interpreting this data through its pyramid of patterns and making decisions regarding what signals to send to its motor outputs that it considers will maximise its physical well-being as denoted by its internal sense-data of pleasure and pain. This forms the foundation for what we might call 'reality' and 'purpose'.

In conclusion, I would like to note that what I am describing are the bare bones of the logic of thinking. There are many details to fill in, in order to improve its accuracy. I would also like to note here that the notion of pattern identification as a core process for constructing a model of the world is self-consistent. It is self-consistent in that the process of pattern identification itself is the most efficient pattern in terms of accuracy and simplicity to fit the relevant data. In fact there is no alternative. The relevant data would include the fact that we humans have a model of the world and the fact that at the start of animal life, our ancestors had no model of the world and the fact that the only portal to the world we have is through our external senses. I would also like to note that the pattern identification process is a strictly logical process, despite its requirement for one or more templates whose form may be somewhat arbitrary or even random. This is because the pattern identification process works as a filter; any templates that don't fit the data are simply discarded.

# Chapter 11
# A Theory of Consciousness

*Our journey now takes us to the wonderful world of consciousness, if we can find it*

In the previous chapters (and summarised in the previous one), we looked at how logical processors can combine sense-data with the process of pattern identification to create a model of the world. The animal's model of the world can then be used to interact with the world via the animal's logical processor which sends signals to its motor outputs that connect to its arms, wings, legs, mouth or whatever. It also gets some feedback from its internal organs, which gives it direction and motivation in terms of maximising pleasure and minimising pain.

In this chapter, I want to extend these ideas a little further. One's model of the world is essentially equivalent to one's pyramid of patterns for it contains all that one knows about the world. The process is perpetually searching for a pattern, a pattern that will compress the data, make sense of the data and simplify one's understanding of the data.

Now suppose that our animal with a logical processor has a good model of the world that enables it to survive and thrive. And the logical processor is always looking to create better patterns of patterns within its pyramid of patterns, especially when it is sleeping.

Then suppose it puts almost everything it knows at the top end of its pyramid of patterns together in one bundle and searches for a pattern that will link them all together. It could take, for example, the patterns regarding the concepts of its physical body; its limbs; the environment of trees, land and sea; the animals it encounters and any other top-end patterns and puts them all together as input in the pattern-identifying process. What might it find? All these concepts seem to be unrelated, but is there a pattern that links them together?

I suggest that there is. I suggest that it is the pattern associated with the concept of 'Me!', 'I am' or 'I exist'.

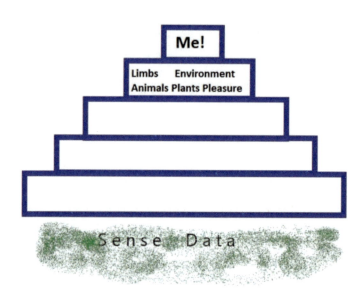

While the pattern which is labelled 'I am' would not be capable of reproducing all the data that it is based upon, it would at the least compress the data. For it provides a simple explanation for all of those seemingly diverse patterns of pleasure, limbs, other animals and so on. It compresses the data as it shows how these diverse patterns can fit together in a cohesive whole instead of being entirely disparate and unconnected patterns.

Once the animal has identified the pattern of 'Me', it would suggest that the animal has become aware of its own existence and achieved what is called 'self-awareness'.

I would like to suggest that the experience of self-awareness for the animal is what we might call 'consciousness'; the awareness of oneself as a vibrant living creature.

The relationship between self-awareness and consciousness is somewhat tenuous; I cannot prove that self-awareness leads to consciousness, and I don't think that anyone can. Consciousness is a very personal experience of self-awareness. Scientists can to some degree test for whether animals have self-awareness through mirrors and paint (on their faces) and such like. Using these tests it can be inferred that a number of species of animals do have self-awareness. From that we can further infer that they also have consciousness; because that would seem to be the experience of self-awareness as it is experienced by a self-aware animal. This consciousness is very special; it is what makes our lives unique.

There is an ephemeral or non-material quality to consciousness. We all experience it, but it cannot be scientifically measured nor even detected.

So on our journey, we have come from a material world to an experience of that material world which is not of itself material, what some might call 'mind'.

The concept of 'self-awareness' that we have arrived at can be said to be 'emergent' from the theory. We have taken just a few simple assumptions, including that of a logical processor, and have arrived at self-awareness. I consider that this is a good indication that we are on the right track in our journey.

It is interesting to note that in popular literature on the topic of consciousness, such as what one might find on the internet or in books, many people suggest that the essence of consciousness is to be found somewhere in the material of the brain, or perhaps in the physics of quantum weirdness and not in simple logic. They seem to think that consciousness is a function of hardware rather than software. But I think they are totally on the wrong track there, and their failure to find consciousness in hardware is evidence for this. Instead, what we have shown here is that consciousness comes from the software of the logic of awareness, from building up a model of the world using little more than sense-data and a logical processor.

This theory of consciousness has implications for the domain of artificial intelligence. Some people have postulated that consciousness will simply appear, once robots or computers reach a sufficient speed and memory and size commensurate with the size of the human brain and that then they will automatically and spontaneously achieve consciousness. Of course, this is entirely illogical. It is nothing more than pure speculation.

To summarise: what we have shown here is that consciousness and self-awareness can be achieved, and perhaps can only be achieved, through the creation of a pyramid of patterns that constitutes a model of the world. That pyramid of patterns arises from the basic logic of pattern identification, combined with external sense-data, combined with physical interaction with the world through motor outputs, arms, legs, feet, etc. and the motivation of pleasure and pain, and which creates a comprehensive model of the world. It is only once that has been achieved, that self-awareness and its associated experience of consciousness can be achieved. For once a high-level pyramid of patterns has been achieved, it is a fairly natural pattern to create the one for the identification of self and one's own existence within the world. This pattern can then be labelled as: 'I am', 'me' or 'I exist'.

It is perhaps interesting to speculate on whether it would ever be possible for an entirely artificial intelligence to achieve consciousness. It would require a computer or robot to have senses, such as for sight and sound, but no installed software other than a pattern-identifying process; it could then be left to run for as long as it takes. Whether anybody would ever want to try to do this is a moot point and perhaps one that is best left for future generations.

# Chapter 12
# The Logic of Decision-Making

*We now venture on our journey into the land of decision-making and the goal of happiness.*

In this chapter, I want to talk about the process of making decisions. This is a follow up to Chapter 10, Foundations of Reality and Purpose.

Decision-making is what the brain does, it is its primary function. It makes decisions so that it can conduct actions, which allow it to interact with the world and to look after its physical body. In order to do this, it creates a model of the world from its sense-data. It has motor outputs, which enable it to interact with the world; it also has internal sense-data, which give it feedback on the physical state of its body. Its internal senses come from all the organs of the body; from the skin, the heart, stomach and even the brain itself.

For the brain is an organ of the body and its well-being is also incorporated into the overall well-being of the body. In earlier chapters, this was just referred to as pleasure and pain, but at this later stage in the development and evolution of our animal, its well-being, as experienced by its brain, can be labelled as 'happiness' or if there is an absence of well-being as 'unhappiness'. This happiness is clearly closely associated with the common usage of the word.

From here on, we will be using the word 'happiness' to indicate the goal to which the logical processor of the brain aspires. This goal incorporates not only short-term experiences of pleasure but also long-term experiences of happiness. The long-term experience of happiness can actually be experienced in the short-term as a feeling of security; that one's long-term goals can be met. For example, a squirrel can experience contentment or happiness at the start of winter, knowing that it has a good supply of hidden nuts to keep it well provided with food over the cold winter months.

It should be noted that what makes a person happy can be specific to that particular person. The requirements of the generalities of food, warmth, shelter, etc. may be universal, but the specifics of what a person's goal of happiness entails will be unique to that particular person and will be determined by a combination of their genetics, their upbringing and their environment. So, for example, some people are more social than others and want to interact co-cooperatively with others, whereas some other people are more solitary.

So how would a logical processor with a good model of the world go about making decisions with the goal of maximising its happiness? First of all, it would assess the situation. It would collate all the possible options for a decision and then examine those options to determine which one would be most likely to maximise its happiness. An important part of this process would be for it to extrapolate aspects of its model of the world into the future so as to indicate the likely consequences of a particular action. It would then estimate the likely happiness or unhappiness of those consequences.

However, in order to combine the possible consequences of a possible decision into just one parameter, the likely happiness of one possible consequence needs to be combined with the likelihood that that consequence will occur. The easiest way to do this is to estimate the probability that this outcome will occur and multiply it by the likely happiness of this particular outcome.

To demonstrate the logic of how this works, the decision-making process can be modelled in the form of an algorithm. To do this it would be necessary to allocate a number to the parameter for the expected happiness. This could be in the range from, say, negative 10 to plus 10, with negative 10 denoting much unhappiness and plus 10 denoting a lot of happiness. These values can be exceeded, if required, to indicate, for example, a complete disaster. These values for happiness might also take into account the time over which the happiness or unhappiness might occur; depending upon whether it is going to be brief, or whether it will last a long time; obviously, greater weight would be given to those that last longer.

The value of this parameter can then be multiplied by an estimate for the probability that this particular outcome will occur. The range of this probability would be from 0 to 1; 0 denoting highly unlikely or impossible, and 1 denoting highly likely or certain. Then for each possible decision the product of the likely happiness and an estimate for the probability for each possible consequence can be added together to give a value for the overall expected happiness associated with that decision.

This process for estimating the expected happiness for a particular decision can be repeated for each possible decision. One can then select the decision that has the greatest expected happiness.

I have drawn up a simple algorithm to indicate how this might work. The algorithm is in a generalised form and can be used for all decisions from what socks to put on in the morning to whether to get married and everything between and beyond.

### Decision-Making Algorithm

1.   Assemble all possible actions for this decision.
2.        Select one possible action.
3.        Assemble all possible consequences of this action.
4.             Select one possible consequence.
5.             Estimate the likelihood or probability that the consequence will occur.
6.             Estimate the happiness (or unhappiness) that one might expect from that consequence in both the short term and the long term. (Use some arbitrary units and put on a scale say from -10 (extreme unhappiness) to +10 (maximum happiness.)

75

7.        Calculate the product of the probability by the estimated happiness to arrive at an overall expected value for the happiness of that consequence.

8.        If there are more possible consequences, loop back to '4', or else, continue.

9.        Add all the expected happiness for each possible consequence together to arrive at a combined expected happiness for this action and store this value alongside a description of the action.

10.       If there are more possible actions, loop back to '2', or else, continue.

11. From the stored values of expected happiness find the one with the highest value.

12. Select the action that is associated with this value.

13. Execute the action.


In essence what this algorithm does is to look at all possible actions and then evaluate all the possible consequences for each of those actions and then select the action which is most likely to bring the most happiness.

It may be helpful to go over an example of how this would work in practice. Imagine, if you will, that you are the captain of a pirate ship, somewhere in the ocean far out to sea, and you detect that you're heading into a storm; you have a decision to make. What are you going to do? Going through the algorithm, you assemble all the possible options. They might include, 'carry on your course', 'head to the nearest port', 'sail away from the storm'.


**Worked Example for Decision-Making Algorithm**

You are the captain of a pirate ship somewhere in the ocean, and you detect that you are heading into a storm.

You have a decision to make:

Option 1: Stay on your course.
Consequences:
(A) Possible damage to ship or sails
(B) Get to destination on time
(C) Complete loss of ship and crew

Option 2: Head to the nearest port.

Consequences:

(A) Port may be unfriendly

(B) Delay in getting to destination

(C) Ship is safe


Option 3: Run away from the storm.

Consequences:

(A) Ship is safe

(B) Delay in getting to destination

(C) Shortage of supplies and unhappy crew


**Option 1: Stay on Your Course**

The possible consequences of carrying on your course might include: possible damage to the ship and sails, get to one's destination on time and the complete loss of ship and crew in the storm. So taking each of those possible consequences in turn; one: possible damage to the ship or sails; maybe you'd give a probability of that occurring as 20%; unhappiness caused perhaps negative 8; to give a total for the product of the probability and the expected happiness as negative 1.6.

(A) Possible damage to ship or sails. P=0.2, H=-8, PxH= **-1.6**

Where P is the estimated probability, H is the estimated happiness and PxH is the product of the two.


Second option: get to the destination on time, likelihood 30%; happiness, say plus eight; taking the product this comes to plus 2.4.

(B) Get to destination on time. P=0.3, H=+8, PxH= **+2.4**


Or the third possibility: complete loss of ship and crew; while it is unlikely maybe 1%, but for the happiness value we're going way over scale and give it a value of minus 100 because it's a complete disaster. Then the product of the happiness and the likelihood, come to negative 1.

(C) Complete loss of ship and crew P=0.01, H=-100, PxH= **-1.0**

So that's all the consequences for that particular action. So then we add those products together, and we get a value of negative 0.2.

Sum of expected happinesses for staying on course: -1.6 +2.4 -1.0 = **-0.2**
So we store that value of -0.2 with the decision to stay on your course.

Then you take the next possible decision: Head to the nearest port. Possible consequences of this might include: the port might be unfriendly, or you are going to be late in getting to your destination but the ship will be safe. The summary might look something like this:

## Option 2: Head to the Nearest Port

Consequences:
(A) Port may be unfriendly. P=0.1, H=-5 PxH= **-0.5**
(B) Delay in getting to destination. P=1.0, H=-2, PxH= **-2.0**
(C) Ship is safe P=0.95, H=+3, PxH= **+2.85**
Sum of expected happinesses for heading to nearest port: -0.5 -2.0 +2.85 = **+0.35**

## Option 3: Sail Away from the Storm

Then considering the third option: Sailing away from the storm. Possible consequences of this might include: the ship may be safe, but you'll be delayed, and there might be other consequences of the delay such as shortage of supplies and an unhappy crew.

Consequences:
(A) Ship is safe. P=0.95, H=+3, PxH= **+2.85**
(B) Delay in getting to destination P=1.0, H=-2, PxH= **-2.0**
(C) Shortage of supplies, unhappy crew P=0.2, H=-4, PxH= **-0.8**
Sum of expected happinesses for staying on course: +2.85 -2.0 -0,8 = **+0.05**

Then, having done that, one can compare the totals for each of those possible actions and select the one with the largest value. Clearly, in this example, with an expected happiness of +0.35, the best decision is to head to the nearest port.

This is, of course, a somewhat idealised algorithm. In practice, there are two major constraints as to its efficiency: first, the accuracy of one's model of the world; the more accurate the model, the more accurate will be one's extrapolation into the future and the more accurate the expected consequences and associated probabilities. Secondly, the time it takes for the brain to work through all the different possibilities; and it may be that it is expedient to make a decision rapidly, in order to meet the particular circumstances.

So if one is out at sea on one's pirate ship, one has to make a decision rapidly. One doesn't want to delay too long for otherwise the storm will hit before one has made a decision. On the other hand, if there's an important decision to be made, where there is no time constraint, it might be beneficial to allow the subconscious brain to work through all the different possible options and consequences; perhaps even during sleep. Hence the common expression for when facing a difficult decision: 'I'll sleep on it'.

One more note on a technical issue: it is not necessary for the probabilities of possible consequences for a particular decision to add to 100%. This is in part because the broad probabilities are only rough estimates. Also, if the estimated happiness of a consequence is zero, or close to zero, i.e. neither happy nor unhappy, it can generally be ignored because the product of the probability and the happiness will be zero.

The reason for putting the decision-making process in the form of an algorithm is to show that it is a logical process and to demonstrate in simple terms how it works.

It should be noted that this account of the decision-making process is descriptive, and not proscriptive. In other words, I'm not saying that people should make decisions to maximise their happiness, I am saying that people do make decisions that seek to maximise their happiness. It is the logical thing to do. This applies to all people for all their decisions.

Some people may deny that they are motivated by happiness; this may be because they have a narrower concept of the meaning of happiness than that which I am using which is essentially the well-being of the physical body. Or perhaps people are simply unaware of the essence of the logic that they are using for decision-making. Or it may just be that they choose to deny it as a way of maximising their own happiness, in other words they want people to believe that they are not motivated by their own personal happiness.

This algorithm for decision-making applies to all animals that have a model of the world, even if it is an extremely rudimentary one. For example, it is applicable to the social insects such as ants and termites when they make decisions to sacrifice themselves in their defence of their nest and queen. For one can infer from their actions of self-sacrifice that the preservation of their nest and queen is paramount to their happiness, where their unique form of happiness will have been created through a process of evolution. For it should be noted that the social insects have a very different reproduction process to that of mammals in that the soldier ants and soldier termites do not reproduce directly, instead reproduction is carried out by their queen. So their sacrifice does not directly affect their ability to reproduce as they have no ability to reproduce directly in the first place.

Every animal has the aim in its decision-making of maximising its own happiness. This is an important principle, and it is emergent from the foundational assumptions of the Pattern Paradigm. This principle is a useful tool for understanding the motivation of not only oneself but also the motivations of other people in what they do and what they say. This can enable one to make better sense of the world. It is not a requirement for the decision-making process to take place at the conscious level of the brain, it can also take place in the subconscious with only the conclusion emerging as a feeling into the conscious.

So does this algorithm fit the facts? It would seem that it does. The decisions and actions of other people are entirely compatible with the idea that they are seeking to maximise their happiness. People may not be aware that this is what they're doing, as the processes of the algorithm may be done in their subconscious, at a level in the brain or pyramid of patterns, that is below the level of consciousness.

Decisions are hugely important; they are what the brain does. The decisions made and the actions taken have real consequences that can have an impact on the rest of one's life. So the quality of those decisions taken will influence the happiness one achieves in the rest of one's life. The quality of decisions will depend upon the accuracy of one's model of the world and also on one's understanding of what will make one happy in the long run and what will not. So it is important to learn the specifics of what will make one personally happy.

It is also important to create an accurate model of the world; and for this it may be necessary to try new and different things and to explore one's environment, both physically and socially. While this may not bring immediate pleasure, it may well improve one's model of the world so that one can make better decisions in the future and in this way, improve one's prospects for long-term happiness.

Finally, I would like to note that despite the paramount importance of decision-making, it is a topic that has largely been ignored by Standard Western Philosophy. This is a failing of SWP and is a major point of difference between SWP and The Pattern Paradigm philosophy that I am describing.

# Chapter 13
# What Is an Abstract System?

*Our journey now takes a slight detour as we turn to explore the domain of abstract systems.*

So far in this philosophical journey we have been following the development of an animal's brain through millions of years of evolution. So having got to the stage of evolution of a few thousand years ago the human brain has become very large, it has got a large capacity for storage of data. It can also process data very rapidly, and it even has spare processing time. It also has a pyramid of patterns and a model of the world with which it interacts with the world. But what else can it do?

One thing it can do is to set up what I am calling an 'abstract system', for which mathematics is just one example. I am calling them abstract systems to differentiate them from real systems. A real system is linked to sense-data and uses a pattern identification process to create a model of the world. An abstract system is entirely abstract, it has no direct links to sense-data and uses its own internal logic to create theorems. An abstract system can only be created by a highly developed brain/mind, and it would also seem to require the ability to write and record symbols.

A 'real' logical system is one that has direct links to sense-data.

An 'abstract' logical system is one that is independent of sense-data.

Without any links to sense-data, an abstract system is necessarily abstract. Yet is is a logical system that has symbols that follow specified rules. Sometimes, the theorems that are generated by an abstract system nay be useful within the real world, or they may just be 'interesting'. (I suggest the pictures at the start of this chapter and the next one, both of which were generated entirely by an abstract system, could be labelled as 'interesting'.)

Mathematics is best understood as a type of abstract system. So before discussing mathematics in particular, I would like to discuss the general form of abstract systems.

The basic requirements for an abstract logical system are three things:

1. Symbols
2. Rules for the manipulation of those symbols
3. Axiom or starting points.
4. It is capable of generating theorems.

A 'theorem' is a string of symbols that can be generated from the rules and the axioms.

It is not hard to create one's own abstract system. I've done so here, where there are some symbols, some rules and an axiom, For this abstract system that I've created there are four symbols: @, #, $ and %. We can label it the abstract system '@#$%'.

Here is a summary of it:

Abstract system @#$%

4 symbols: @, #, $, %

**Rules of the System:**

1.  The string '%@' can be replaced by '@'
2.  For a string that has a '$' symbol in it, the string '@%' may be added to the beginning <u>and</u> '%@' to the end.
3.  The string '@@@@@' may be replaced by '#', and vice versa.

NB 'String' refers to a sequence of one or more symbols.

What this system does is manipulate strings of symbols according to specific rules.

So, now, we want to create theorems from this system. We can start with an axiom of '@$@' and then select which rules we want to apply in order to generate theorems. (Note that each theorem generated acts as a starting point for the subsequent one.)

Axiom: @$@
Theorems:
@%@$@%@ (by rule 2)
@%@$@@ (by rule 1)
@%@%@$@@%@ (rule 2)
@%@%@$@@@ (rule 1)
@%@%@%@$@@@%@ (rule 2)
@%@%@%@$@@@@ (rule 1)
@%@%@%@%@$@@@@@%@ (rule 2)
@%@%@%@%@$@@@@@ (rule 1)
@%@%@%@%@$# (rule 3)

This is an example of a simple and perhaps trivial abstract system. It has symbols, rules of inference, an axiom, and it can generate theorems.

So does the final theorem: '@%@%@%@%@$#' 'mean' anything? Could it be useful in some way? Is it 'interesting'?

As I have shown, it is easy to create an abstract system that is capable of generating theorems. The hard part is creating an abstract system that is 'interesting' in some way or other. What does 'interesting' mean? 'Interesting' means that it stimulates brain activity; this could mean that it is possible to correlate some of the symbols with the patterns from the real world, i.e. the patterns within the pyramid of patterns that we have in our own heads.

We will be coming back to these theorems, but first I want to take a different tack and look at some simple sense-data. So this is for processing in the real world using the normal pattern identification process.

Suppose you are presented with the following data strings:

| | |
|---|---|
| AFG | BRT |
| LMQ | PPR |
| AAN | TOJ |

And then I ask you which of the following strings fits best, with the ones above?

1. FF
2. B
3. AZWY
4. FRZT
5. NPZ

Of the five different options, I'm sure you'll have no difficulty in identifying the last one NPZ as being the one that fits best with that other group. And why? Well, because you will have identified a concept, the idea of 'threeness', each of them has three different symbols in it. And you've created the idea of three symbols and so the option that has three symbols is the one that fits best with the others. This concept of 'three' is a pattern We have a concept of 'three' in the same way that we have a concept of 'yellow' or 'loud'. This 'three' is often associated with the symbol '3', especially in the logical system of mathematics. But it is a slightly different three because one is purely a symbol within the system of mathematics and the other is a label for a pattern for the concept of threeness. I distinguish between them by writing one as 'three' and the other as a simple '3'.

'Three' is a label for a pattern.

The '3' is a symbol within the system of mathematics.

Going back to the abstract system we had before of the system #@$%. I used these symbols to highlight the abstractness of the system; they are just purely random symbols; which means that I can simply change them if I want to and nothing regarding the quality of the abstract system is changed. So perhaps, instead of writing '@', I can write '1', instead of '#', 'V' instead of '$', '=' and instead of '%', '+'. Then when these symbols are substituted into the system, it becomes:

Abstract system 1V=+
4 symbols: 1 V = +

**Rules of the System:**

1. The string '+1' can be replaced by '1'
2. For a string that has a '=' symbol in it, the string '1+' may be added to the beginning <u>and</u> '+1' to the end.
3. The string '11111' may be replaced by 'V', and vice versa.

NB 'String' refers to a sequence of one or more symbols.
Axiom: 1=1
Theorems:
1+1=1+1 (by rule 2)
1+1=11 (by rule 1)
1+1+1=11+1 (rule 2)
1+1+1=111 (rule 1)
1+1+1+1=111+1 (rule 2)
1+1+1+1=1111 (rule 1)
1+1+1+1+1=1111+1 (rule 2)
1+1+1+1+1=11111 (rule 1)
1+1+1+1+1=V (rule 3)

The symbols of these theorems can be recognised as mapping onto a simple counting system. It is essentially what would be called a 'base 1' system and which was used by the ancient Romans. (They used 'V' as an abbreviation for '11111'.) So effectively, what we have is an abstract system, which adds five ones together and gets a symbol V. The effect of changing those symbols is that those symbols that are '1' and '+' and '=' and 'V' can be recognised as having meaning within the pyramid of patterns; we can map from one system to the other so that the symbols are not isolated solely within the logical abstract system.

The relationship between the two systems, one abstract and one real, can be best described as a 'mapping' and there is a mapping between the symbols of the abstract system and the labels for patterns. So '1', as a symbol, we can associate with a concept of 'oneness'. The '=' symbol we can associate with the concept of 'equals' and so on.

One other point to note is that applying the rules of an abstract system or running the algorithms to generate theorems requires the use of a brain/mind that understands the rules, such as a person. The person can then either run the rules themselves, perhaps on a piece of paper, or they can design and manufacture a machine which will do it for them, such as a computer.

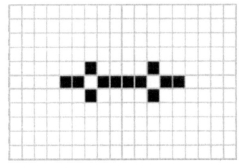

Looking now at other abstract systems:

An example of a different abstract system is Conway's Game of Life, which has symbols, i.e black and white squares; it has rules, and it has an axiom i.e. the starting point. And then it goes through a sequence of different applications of the rules to end up in different configurations, or theorems.

Conway's Game of Life can be considered to be an abstract system, it's a little bit different to the others because the rules are very specific, and they are applied exactly the same way each time it completes a cycle. Whereas in maths or in other abstract systems, there are different rules and one can choose which rule to apply, depending on what one wants to achieve.

Another type of abstract system is the game of chess.

It has symbols, i.e. all the different pieces; it has rules which are very specific, and it has an axiom i.e. the starting position for all the different symbols. It is different to the other ones because there are two players, each trying to use the rules in a specific way to achieve a particular goal. Each of the different players has a different goal in mind, and they are competing against each other, and it is a game. Nevertheless, it is a type of abstract system.

I am mentioning these abstract systems to show that there are other interesting abstract systems besides mathematics. I created the abstract system @#$% to show how easy it is to set up a viable abstract system that can generate theorems.

We will discuss the abstract system of mathematics in the next chapter.

# Chapter 14
# The Foundation of Mathematics

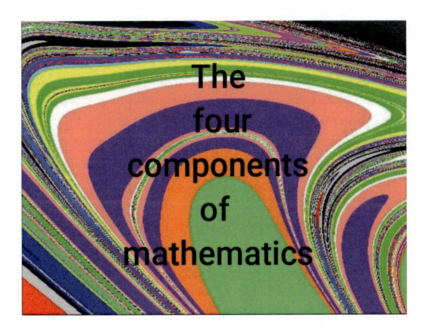

*Our journey now takes us to the abstract mountain of mathematics; we will ascend a little way... but we won't go far.*

What is wanted from a philosophy of mathematics? What is required is an explanation for how its logic works and how it fits in with the rest of philosophical knowledge.

In the previous chapter, we discussed how abstract systems can be created. Pure mathematics is clearly an abstract system. It has symbols, rules, axioms and theorems.

We shall begin our exploration of mathematics by examining its logic and how it works.

Going back to the very beginning of maths, around the time of our hunter-gatherer ancestors, it would have started with just mere scratchings on a cave wall or a piece of wood, with a series of 1's; essentially, base 1 arithmetic. The example I gave in the previous chapter where we had the abstract system '1V=+' which generated the theorem: 1+1+1+1+1=V, is essentially base 1 arithmetic, where each 1 represents 1 and nothing more. I'm using base 1 arithmetic here because it's the most simple, and it is the basis for all arithmetic. What we are doing here is looking at the foundations of mathematics, what it is and how it works.

The mathematics we generally use today uses base 10; i.e. it uses 10 symbols from 0 to 9 to represent the numbers. Computers use binary (base 2) notation which has just two symbols 0 and 1. It is a fairly straightforward procedure to convert base 10 numbers to base 2 and vice versa. Less common is the unary system or base 1. However, it is the system that the ancient Romans used. They used the letters V, X, L and C as well to abbreviate the numbers, but it was still essentially a base 1 system.

Mathematics was created all those years ago as a means of recording numbers of objects. There could be a direct and simple mapping between the number of marks (1's) and the number of objects. Mathematics is still taught this way as a correlation between numbers and actual objects.

Within base 1 arithmetic, it is very easy to see the correspondence between the symbols and the reality. It is interesting to note that ancient shepherds could keep track of the number of sheep that they possessed without recourse to actual counting. All they would need to do is to make a mark, such as a '1' on a piece of wood or similar for each of the sheep in their flock before heading out to the pastures. Then on their return they could see if each mark on the piece of wood still corresponded to an individual sheep. Then if there is one more mark than sheep they can conclude that one sheep has been lost somewhere. (Nowadays, this would be called using a 'tally-stick'.)

IIII

There is a mapping between each mark on a piece of wood and the shepherd's concept of 'one sheep'.

However, when exploring the philosophy of mathematics, it is useful to separate the symbolic maths from the real world objects and treat them entirely independently; in other words we shall separate pure maths from applied maths. So then there is pure maths which is the manipulation of abstract symbols in a logical abstract system and applied maths which uses a mapping from those abstract symbols to real-world objects and real world phenomena.

I want to show how pure mathematics is the manipulation of symbols, according to specified rules, to produce theorems and nothing more. There is no inherent meaning to it, they are just meaningless symbols that are manipulated to produce theorems, which may be interesting because they can be mapped onto the real world. To show how the symbols can be manipulated, I will go over a few examples using base 1 arithmetic; where one only has strings of '1's or possibly an empty string.

It is fairly straightforward to convert base 1 numbers to base 2 and vice versa or on to base 10 as required. What I want to do here is to show how strings of base 1 numbers can be manipulated to satisfy the basic operations of mathematics. I am using base 1 arithmetic to demonstrate how the symbols can be manipulated because it is much simpler than using higher base arithmetic as there is no concern about the specific position of a symbol in a string as all the symbols are the same, which is not the case for higher base arithmetic.

An algorithm is a set of rules for generating a theorem.

**Elementary Maths system.**
Symbols:1, +, -, /, *
Rules: Algorithms for 'plus', 'minus', 'times' and 'divide'.
Axioms: Any string of 1's.

So if one wants to add two base 1 numbers together or base 1 strings, there is a simple algorithm that one can use. I will put one here:

**Addition**: To add Strings S1 and S2 together and put the sum in S3
Set S3 = empty
Add S1 to RHS of S3
Add S2 to RHS of S3

Output S3

S1, S2 and S3 are simply labels for strings. That's all they are (RHS = Right Hand Side). And 'empty' denotes that the string is empty or contains no symbols.

One can see how this works in an example:

Worked example: Add 111 to 11 (Set S1 to '111'and S2 to '11')

| S1 | S2 | S3 | |
|----|----|----|----|
| 111 | 11 | | (Initial conditions) |
| 111 | 11 | 111 | (Adding S1 to RHS of S3) |
| 111 | 11 | 11111 | (Adding S2 to RHS of S3) |
| Output 11111 | | | (Outputting S3) |

(In base 10, this is adding 3 to 2 to get 5 or 3+2=5).

This output theorem is interesting because it matches what we know about the real world, where the concept of 'two' combines with the concept of 'three' to give the concept of 'five'.

One can use another algorithm for 'subtraction'. Should one want to subtract S2 from S1, here is an algorithm for that:

**Subtraction**: Subtract S2 from S1 and return a '-' sign with the string if S2 is greater than S1

|   |   |
|---|---|
|   | Set Ss = empty |
| A | If S2 is empty Goto C |
|   | If S1 is empty Goto B |
|   | Remove last (RHS) symbol of S2 |
|   | Remove last (RHS) symbol of S1 |
|   | Goto A |
| B | If S2 is not empty Set Ss to '-' |
|   | Set S1 equal to S2 |
| C | Output: Ss S1 |

Note that this one returns a negative sign if the length of the string S2 is longer than the string S1. So if one were wanting to subtract four from three, it will return -1. The 'negative' sign, if required, is stored in Ss.

Worked example: Subtract 11 from 1111 (Set S2 to '11' and S1 to '1111').

| S1 | S1 | Ss | |
|----|----|----|----|
| 1111 | 11 | | (Initial conditions) |
| 111 | 1 | | (Removing last symbols of S2 and S1) |
| 11 | | | (Removing last symbols of S2 and S1) |
| Output 11 | | | (Outputting Ss S1) |

So, in this example, subtracting '11' from '1111' produces the output '11' (or in base 10: 4-2=2).

Second worked example: Subtract 1111 from 11

| S1 | S2 | Ss | |
|----|----|----|----|
| 11 | 1111 | | (Initial conditions) |
| 1 | 111 | | (Removing last symbols of S2 and S1) |
| | 11 | | (Removing last symbols of S2 and S1) |
| 11 | 11 | - | (Setting S1 equal to S2 and Ss to '-') |
| Output: - 11 | | | (Outputting Ss S1) |

So, in this example, if one subtracts '1111' from '11', it outputs '-11'. (In base 10, this is 2-4=-2.)

The negative symbol is just a symbol, it means nothing within the abstract system of pure mathematics, but in the real world, we can associate that symbol as being 'negative'.

Then there is an algorithm for the multiplication of two numbers or of two strings:

**Multiplication**: Multiply S1 by S2 and output the product in S3

    Set S3 = empty

A    Add S1 to RHS of S3

    Remove last symbol of S2

    If S2 is not empty then Goto A

    Output S3

Here is a worked example:

Worked Example: Multiply 111 by 11

| S1 | S1 | S3 | |
|----|----|----|----|
| 111 | 11 | | (Initial conditions) |
| 111 | 1 | 111 | (Adding S1 to S3 and removing last symbol of S2) |
| 111 | | 111111 | (Adding S1 to S3 and removing last symbol of S2) |
| Output 111111 | | | (Outputting S3) |

So 'multiplying' '111' by '11' generates an output of '111111'. Or in base 10 this is 3*2=6.

Note that when I'm doing this, there is no use of number within the algorithms, I am merely manipulating the strings; nothing more; i.e. adding a symbol here, taking one off there, that is all. There is no concept of number, it's just a manipulation of strings. I could just as easily have used the symbols from the abstract system @#$% instead of the 1, +, -, /, * of this system; the logic and application would have remained unchanged.

Here is an algorithm for division. Division can be associated with repeated subtraction, and so this one uses the subtraction algorithm used previously:

**Division**: Divide S1 by S2 and return a fractional part if the numbers do not divide exactly.

      Set S3 = empty

      Set Ss = empty

      Set S4 equal to S2

      If S2 is empty, then output 'ERROR' and then Stop.

A      Subtract S2 from S1 (Using the subtraction algorithm that returns Ss and S1)

      Set S2 equal to S4 (this just resets the value of S2 after it is altered in the subroutine)

      If Ss = '-' Goto B

      Add a '1' to the RHS of S3

      If S1 is not empty Goto A

      Output S3

      Stop

B      Set S2 = S1

      Set S1 = S4

      Subtract S2 from S1 (using the subtraction algorithm)

      Output S3 + S1/S4

      Stop

It shows how S1 can be 'divided' by S2. using nothing more than string manipulation. It is reasonably comprehensive in that it returns a fractional part if the numbers do not divide exactly (The string 'S1/S2' can be mapped onto a fraction in the real world). It also returns an output of 'ERROR' if S2, the 'divisor', is empty.

Here are some examples of how the different strings change as one proceeds through the algorithm.

**Example:** Divide 111111 by 11

| S1 | S2 | S3 | S4 | Ss | |
|---|---|---|---|---|---|
| 111111 | 11 | | 11 | | (Initial conditions) |
| 1111 | 11 | 1 | 11 | | (Subtracting S2 from S1 and adding '1' to RHS of S3) |
| 11 | 11 | 11 | 11 | | (Subtracting S2 from S1 and adding '1' to RHS of S3) |
| | 11 | 111 | 11 | | (Subtracting S2 from S1 and adding '1' to RHS of S3) |
| Output 111 | | | | | (Outputting S3) |

So if one 'divides' '111111' by '11', the output ls the string '111'.

(In base 10 this is 6/2=3)

**Second worked example:** Divide 11111 by 11

| S1 | S2 | S3 | S4 | Ss | |
|---|---|---|---|---|---|
| 11111 | 11 | | 11 | | (Initial conditions) |
| 111 | 11 | 1 | 11 | | (Subtracting S2 from S1 and adding '1' to RHS of S3) |
| 1 | 11 | 11 | 11 | | (Subtracting S2 from S1 and adding '1' to RHS of S3) |
| 1 | 11 | 11 | 11 | - | (Subtracting S2 from S1 makes Ss negative) |
| 1 | 1 | 11 | 11 | - | (Setting S2=S1) |
| 11 | 1 | 11 | 11 | | (Setting S1=S4) |
| 1 | 1 | 11 | 11 | | (Subtracting S2 from S1) |
| Output 11 + 1/11 | | | | | (Outputting S3 + S2/S4) |

So if one 'divides' '11111' by '11', the output is '11 +1/11'.

(in base 10 this is 5÷2=2 ½)

**Third worked example:** Divide 11111111 by 111

| S1 | S2 | S3 | S4 | Ss | |
|---|---|---|---|---|---|
| 11111111 | 111 | | 111 | | (Initial conditions) |
| 11111 | 111 | 1 | 111 | | (Subtracting S2 from S1 and adding '1' to RHS of S3) |
| 11 | 111 | 11 | 111 | | (Subtracting S2 from S1 and adding '1' to RHS of S3) |
| 1 | 1 | 11 | 111 | - | (Subtracting S2 from S1 makes Ss 'negative') |
| 111 | 1 | 11 | 111 | | (Setting S2=S1) |
| 111 | 1 | 11 | 111 | - | (Setting S1=S4) |

| 11 | 1 | 11 | 111 | (Subtracting S2 from S1) |

Output: 11+11/111                      (Outputting S3 + S1/S4)

So if one 'divides' the string '11111111' by the string '111', the algorithm outputs the string '11+11/111'. (Or in base 10 this is $8 \div 3 = 2\ \frac{2}{3}$.)

This demonstrates how base 1 arithmetic can be used to denote fractions and by extrapolation all rational numbers.

And you might ask: What does base 1 arithmetic have to do with ordinary mathematics, where we generally use base 10? Well, it is quite simple; again using only the manipulation of strings, we can convert base 1 strings to base 2 strings.

Here is an algorithm that will convert base 1 numbers to base 2:

**Algorithm for converting Base 1 to Base 2** arithmetic, using only the manipulation of strings:

For the conversion of unary to binary numbers we shall require the use of an additional symbol: '0'

S0, S1, S2. S3 are stores for strings of symbols.

Let S0 = the base 1 string to be converted

Set S1 = empty, S2 = empty, S3 = empty

Set S1 = S0

A      If S1 = empty then add a '0' to LHS of S2 then goto B

If S1 = 1 then

          Add a '1' to LHS of S2

          Goto B

Else

Remove last (RHS) symbol of S1

Remove last (RHS) symbol of S1 (this is a repeated operation)

Add a '1' to LHS of S3

Goto A

B      If S3 is <u>not</u> empty then

          Set S1 = S3

          Set S3 = empty

          Goto A

Else

Output: S0 base 1 converts to S2 base 2

Stop

Here is a worked example of how the number 11111 base 1 converts to 101 base two.

**Worked example**: Convert 11111 base 1 to base 2

| S0 | S1 | S2 | S3 | |
|---|---|---|---|---|
| 11111 | | | | Initial conditions |
| 11111 | 11111 | | | Set S1 to S0 |
| 11111 | 111 | | 1 | Removing last 2 symbols of S1 and adding a '1' to LHS of S3) |
| 11111 | 1 | | 11 | Removing last 2 symbols of S1 and adding a '1' to LHS of S3 |
| 11111 | 1 | 1 | 11 | Adding a '1' to LHS of S2 |
| 11111 | 11 | 1 | | Setting S1 = S3 and then S3 = empty |
| 11111 | | 1 | 1 | Removing last 2 symbols of S1 and adding a '1' to LHS of S3 |
| 11111 | | 01 | 1 | Adding a '0' to LHS of S2 |
| 11111 | 1 | 01 | | Setting S1 = S3 and then S3 = empty |
| 11111 | 1 | 101 | | Adding a '1' to LHS of S2 |

11111 base 1 converts to 101 base 2' (Output: S0 base 1 converts to S2 base 2)

So they're both 5 (that is '5' in base 10). So that '5' in base 1 converts to '5' in base 2.

If the unary number that one wants to convert to binary contains fractions, one can simply convert the numerator and the denominator separately.

Then having got to base 2, one can, of course, convert to base 10; there are a lot of algorithms around that will do this as it is commonly taught in secondary schools.

I've gone over this base 1 arithmetic in some detail because there is very little in the literature or on the internet about how base 1 arithmetic works.

I have shown how mathematics in general and arithmetic in particular can be logically developed from its origins as scratches on a piece of wood.

So what we have discussed is the start of mathematics; the foundations of mathematics. It is also the start of understanding mathematics as the manipulation of strings of abstract symbols.

This is also evidenced by the fact that pocket calculators and computers can do arithmetic. They use simple algorithms and manipulate strings, entirely oblivious of any meaning. The strings and symbols mean nothing to them, beyond perhaps selecting the rules to be applied to generate their theorems.

It is only when that output is taken and put across to a person's pyramid of patterns that we can ascribe some meaning to it when we associate the output with our concept of 'numbers', the concept of 'equals' and other concepts.

It is interesting to note that intrinsically, within an abstract system, there is no requirement for what is called 'consistency', this is because the symbols are inherently meaningless. The only expectation of consistency comes when one examines how one might map a theorem to the real world and then one can explore whether it makes sense in the real world.

So, for example, if the string or theorem came along of '1=2' simply by following the rules of the system... What then? The string '1 = 2' doesn't map well to the concepts that we have of the world, given the typical mapping between numbers and our concepts. Our concept of 'one' is quite different to the concept of 'two' and we don't like to think that 'one' equals 'two', and so we don't like it when our mathematics produces the string '1=2'. Yet this can happen using simple algebra:

**'Proof' that 1 = 2**

| Let | $a$ | = | $b$ | |
|---|---|---|---|---|
| Then | $a^2$ | = | $ab$ | multiplying each side by a |
| then | $a^2-b^2$ | = | $ab-b^2$ | subtracting $b^2$ from each side |
| then | $(a+b)(a-b)$ | = | $b(a-b)$ | factorising each side |
| then | $a+b$ | = | $b$ | dividing each side by (a-b) |
| then | $b+b$ | = | $b$ | substituting a for b since a = b) |
| then | $2b$ | = | $b$ | combining terms |
| then | $2$ | = | $1$ | dividing each side by b |
| or | $1$ | = | $2$ | |

(This proof is well-known and easily found in the literature, I am only including details of it here for completeness.)

So to avoid this inconsistency mathematicians put in a rule that you're not allowed to divide by zero. While this rule may seem to be somewhat arbitrary and contrived, it does succeed in invalidating the 'proof' of 1 = 2. (In line 4 of the 'proof' above there is a division by a-b when a=b and thus a-b is zero and thus this line is considered invalid.)

The thing about abstract systems is that they are totally logical and totally rigorous, within the rules of the system. It's not like the real world where one has sense-data coming in, and it's not quite clear what that sense-data is and one is not quite sure what is the best pattern that fits the data.

In an abstract system, it is totally rigorous. As previously mentioned, one has symbols, rules, axioms and theorems; and those are totally rigid. Many people think that mathematics is necessarily 'true' because within that system, one can prove theorems in the way that we just proved that '1+1+1+1+1 = 5'. One can also prove that '1+1 = 2' and it is also totally rigorous within that system. Some people like to say that means it is 'true', but if it is 'true', then it is only 'true' within that particular logical system.

It's only 'true' for the particular use of those symbols and using those particular rules; so it is totally rigorous and 'true' but only within that particular abstract system. This is the case for the mathematics abstract system too; what is logically proven within that system is logically 'true' but only within the system of mathematics.

There seem to be four distinct components of mathematics: Pure maths, Applied maths, Design maths and Pattern maths.

1.  **Pure maths**: The manipulation of symbols according to the rules of the system to generate theorems.

This is what we talked about before and which is exclusively concerned with the symbols, the rules, the axioms and the theorems. And it is all totally meaningless. It is only concerned with the manipulation of strings of symbols. They are just strings, they have no intrinsic meaning. There is no question about consistency or anything like that; whatever the rules dictate that is how the theorems are generated within the particular system of pure mathematics.

What is variable in the system of mathematics is how and where those rules are applied, in which order, and with what axioms one might want to apply. So, for example, if one has simultaneous equations as one's input one can choose which rules to use to manipulate those equations to get to where one wants, i.e. to a 'solution' of the equations.

2.  **Applied Maths:** The application of pure maths to the real world by means of a mapping.

One of the problems with the standard version of the philosophy of mathematics is that people conflate pure maths with applied maths, and this creates confusion. For the two need to be treated quite separately. As Einstein once wrote: "So far as the propositions of mathematics are certain, they do not refer to reality; and so far as they refer to reality, they are not certain." So pure mathematics is certain with its rigorous axioms and rules of inference, but to apply it to the real world requires a subjective mapping, which is not rigorous, and hence, the certainty is removed.

Suppose we have a field of grass and want to know what the area of the field is. What we can do is to map between measured dimensions of the field in the real world with particular symbols or numbers in the abstract domain. Then those numbers can be manipulated in the abstract world to arrive at a conclusion which can then be mapped back to the real world.

Suppose, for example, the field one wants to know the area of is rectangular. One can proceed by measuring the length and breadth of the field in some arbitrary units, say metres. One can then take these pure numbers that represent the length and breadth of the field and map them into the system of mathematics. One can then follow the algorithm for multiplication to multiply those two numbers together. One can then map this number back into the real world and ascribe it squared units, such as square metres, to arrive at a good estimate for the area of the rectangular field.

But the mapping between the abstract world and the real world is not always obvious. So, for example, if one is counting sheep, one has $1+1=2$ and one can map that to 1 sheep + 1 sheep = 2 sheep. But if one has drops of water, like one drop of water plus one drop of water generally doesn't produce two drops of water; it just produces one slightly larger drop of water. If one wanted to model the motion of a ball travelling through the air, then one doesn't want to use statistics or matrices, what one wants to use is calculus.

Please note that when I use the term 'real world', I am referring to the model of the world that we have in our minds and which was created through a process of pattern identification and is contained in our pyramid of patterns, as discussed in previous chapters.

Mathematics is incredibly complex. While we can learn the game of Conway's Game of Life or chess in a few minutes; it takes 10 or more years in school to learn mathematics. Even then, one only learns a small portion of mathematics. It is very, very complex but extremely useful, particularly in its mapping of statistics, physics, finance and all those sorts of things. This complexity can be seen in the rather complex algorithms that we looked at earlier for the comparatively straightforward operations of addition, subtraction, multiplication and division.

3. **Design Maths:** The design of the abstract system, including the creation of the rules and symbols.

This is the where the rules for the mathematical system are chosen which determine how the symbols are manipulated within the abstract system. It is where the rules are selected or designed, for example, for solving differential equations, simple algebra and geometry. What are the rules? How can the rules be designed so that the theorems can be mapped in a meaningful way to the real world?

So there is a lot in the design of the pure mathematical abstract system to arrange it so that many of its theorems can be mapped to a model of the real world. Mathematics is specifically designed and has specific rules so that it can be used to model the real world. (Included within the design is the rule of the non-legality of division by zero, as discussed earlier.)

Also, within the design of maths, one has to invent new symbols. For example, calculus uses specific symbols that are different to any other. There is also a special symbol (i) that is used to designate the square root of negative 1. It is a very useful symbol, but it had to be designed.

It also had to be designed as to how that symbol and its associated rules can be brought into the system of mathematics without creating a contradiction. (A contradiction being something which does not match with the real world). While the square root of negative 1 is called 'imaginary', it is no more imaginary than ordinary integers. You can count sheep using integers 1, 2, 3, 4, 5; or if you wanted to, you could count them using imaginary numbers of $1i$, $2i$, $3i$, $4i$ etc. (where 'i' represents $\sqrt{-1}$), it makes no difference, it is just a different mapping.

4. **Pattern Mathematics:** The application of pattern identification logic to the theorems of maths to search for patterns and ask questions.

This component of mathematics is really just for mathematicians. Mathematicians look at the whole system of mathematics and look for patterns within the theorems.

One can look at all the theorems of maths and then search for a pattern, using a pattern-identifying process. Then one can ask questions such as: 'Are there a finite number of prime numbers?'; 'Is there a solution to the equation: $A^3 + B^3 = C^3$, where A, B and C are integers?' and other questions like those. Mathematicians enjoy playing around with questions like these; they explore the whole system of mathematics. But this is not directly related to the other three components of mathematics.

It is interesting to note that this approach to the philosophy of maths is entirely consistent with Gödel's Incompleteness Theorem. His theorem entailed making the assumptions that mathematics was 'complete' and that one can make statements about mathematics that are not theorems, but which can be designated as being 'true'. He then found that there was an inconsistency. This then implied that at least one of the assumptions was incorrect. The one normally taken to be incorrect is that of completeness; i.e. the system of mathematics is not 'complete'. Some people consider that to be a problem, but within the approach to mathematics that I have been describing, it is not a problem at all. There's no question about whether the system of mathematics is complete or not; it just is what it is.

The only place that truth appears within this approach to mathematics occurs when a theorem is generated and then that theorem can be considered to be 'true' within the system and one can then label it, if one so wants, as 'true'.

So I am claiming that this approach to the philosophy of mathematics within the overall philosophy of The Pattern Paradigm is simple, comprehensive and accurate.

This is in contrast to the Standard Western philosophy approach, which is, to say the least, problematic. The difficulty that SWP has is that they do not distinguish between pure maths and applied maths; they conflate the two together. This problem of conflation is akin to trying to find the foundations of a person together with the clothes they are wearing, but instead of treating them as two different entities they treat them as though they are just one entity; and of course this does not work. Bertrand Russell and others tried to prove that 1+1 = 2 was a consequence of pure logic; and, of course, it didn't work. Now other people try to claim that mathematics can be deduced from sets, thinking that sets are somehow more fundamental than integers. All they have really shown is that there is a correspondence between sets on one hand and pure numbers on the other; they haven't shown that one is more fundamental than the other.

*Well that is as far as we need to go up the mountain of mathematics. We have found the foundations of mathematics and how maths can be mapped onto the real world. We can leave the rest of the exploration of the mountain of mathematics to mathematicians.*

# Chapter 15
# The Real Philosophy of Science (and Its Implications for Quantum Weirdness)

*Our journey now takes us into the domain of science, the branch of philosophy that has been so successful where we shall explore its foundations and logical processes.*

In this chapter, I want to look at science or more specifically the philosophy of science. It is the branch of philosophy that has been supremely successful in transforming our world from that of a hunter-gatherer to that of our modern technological marvels.

What does one want from a philosophy of science? Similarly to other branches of philosophy, what is required is a description of how its logic works and how it fits in with other philosophical knowledge.

So what is the essential process of science that has made it so effective?

In essence the process of science is a continuation of the logical processes that were described earlier by which pattern identification of sense-data is used to build a pyramid of patterns and a model of the world.

However, there are two main differences:

1. While the pattern identification process used for perception is mostly effected in the subconscious part of the mind, science is conducted entirely in the upper conscious part of the mind.

2 While perception is mostly a passive process in that data simply arrives at our senses, in science data is typically actively sought through experiments or observations using specialised equipment.

So, for example, the non-scientific normative view of the world looks for simple patterns in the physical world and finds that the Earth is flat, the Sun goes around the Earth and a constant force on a cart produces a constant speed. But science has sought data beyond the normative domain and has shown that there are better patterns that can be found that describe the same data. Science has found that the Earth is a sphere, the Earth goes around the Sun and that a constant force on a cart produces a constant acceleration (when friction and air resistance are taken into account) and that these constitute better patterns to fit the data than the normative ones.

Nevertheless, despite these differences, the logical process of inference is essentially the same.

In Chapter 8, I introduced an algorithm to describe how information can be gleaned from sense-data with no prior assumptions as to the nature of the sense-data. The essence of this logic. Here is that algorithm:

**Simple Algorithm for Pattern Identification**
1. Assemble the data.
2. Input a template.
3. Test the template—does it fit?
4. If it does not fit go to step 2
5. Else continue
6. Store the template together with a label for the data.

From a logical perspective, the aim of the algorithm is to compress the data. In order to do this one needs to find a pattern that can be described in a more compact form than that of the raw data itself. There is also the requirement that the pattern fits the data and can be used to reproduce the data.

The purpose of putting the process in the form of an algorithm is to demonstrate that it is a logical process.

In this chapter, I want to discuss this algorithm in more detail and to see how it can apply to science. So I have put together a more detailed algorithm.

### More Detailed Pattern-Identifying Algorithm:

1. Assemble the data and give it a label.
2. Select a template. (This can be random or a section of the data or one previously identified.)
3. Apply and expand the template to the data.
4. Measure the differences between the applied pattern and the original data.
5. Sum the differences.
6. Store the template and the sum of the differences.
7. Are there other templates to test? If 'yes', go to step 2; otherwise, continue.
8. Of all the templates tested, select the one with the least sum of differences.
9. Store this template in association with the label for the original data.

Some notes on the algorithm:

**Line one: Assemble the data and give it a label.** The assembled data would need to have something in common with all the other bits of data. The range of the data defines the domain of the pattern.

**Line 2: Select a template.** This is perhaps the most interesting part of the algorithm, for it requires what might be called 'imagination' to concoct a possible template for the pattern. A template is a possible pattern; it is what will be tested to see if it fits the data. It can be anything at all; there is no limit to what could act as a template. It could be entirely random, or it could be a section of the data, or it could be a template from an entirely different domain, or it could be a combination of two or more different templates.

Examples of templates put in a mathematical form might be '$y = x$', '$y = 3x$', '$y = x^2+2$', etc.

105

**Line 3: Apply and expand the template to the data**. To show how this works I have put together some data, which is displayed in a two-dimensional form.

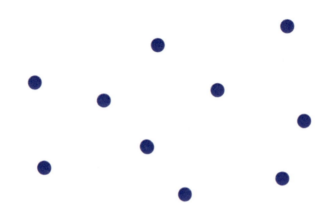

Here, the data is a little more than a scatter diagram, but it will suffice for this example.

Then suppose that the first template is something like y equals x, which can be represented by a diagonal line.

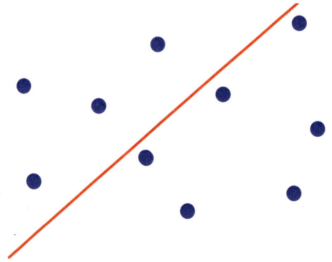

So this diagram shows how the proposed pattern would look within the domain of the data.

**Line 4: Measure the difference between the applied pattern and the original data.** So what you can do here is to drop perpendicular lines from the data points to the proposed pattern as in the diagram.

In this way, one can get an indication of the differences between the data and the pattern.

**Line 5: Sum the differences.** When one has obtained the differences, one can then add all the lengths of the differences to get an overall indication of how accurate the pattern is. This could possibly be refined by using the squares of the differences or using some other analytic method of assessing the accuracy of the pattern, but for this example, we will just add up all the lengths of the differences.

**Line 6: Store the template and the sum of the differences.** One needs to store this information because it will be used later.

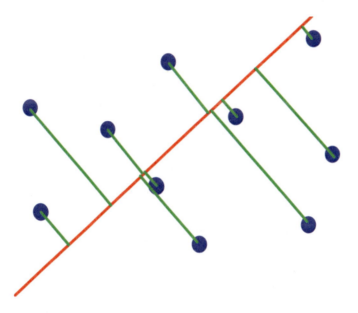

**Line 7: Are there any other templates to test?** So now one can test other templates, such as $y = 2x$, or $y = x^2$, and repeat the process of applying each template to the data, looking at the differences, summing up the differences and then storing the sum of the differences alongside the details of the pattern. If there are no more templates to test, then continue to line 8.

**Line 8: Of all the templates tested select the one with the least sum of differences**. So here one selects the template that best fits the data. In order to do that, one searches through all the stored sums of differences to find the least sum. Then one takes this template with the least differences as being the best available pattern.

**Line 9: Store this 'best pattern' in association with the label for the original data.** So one ends up with the best pattern stored alongside the label for the domain of the data.

This algorithm, or at least a variation of it, lies at the heart of the scientific process. I have shown a fairly generalised form of the algorithm of the scientific process. It can be modified so that it can be applied to any branch of science.

Also, I have portrayed this algorithm using only the criteria of accuracy to determine which pattern to select, but there is also the criteria of the simplicity of the pattern. This could be used if no pattern stands out as being clearly better than the others using the criteria of accuracy alone. (The simpler the pattern, the greater the data compression.)

Sometimes a particular pattern will fit the data exceptionally well and no other pattern fits the data at all well. In this case, the pattern can be used with confidence.

For example, Newton's laws of motion are highly accurate in determining the motions of matter. In other domains, no particular pattern might stand out above the others. As for example, in trying to determine the connections and family tree of early hominids.

The other thing that science can do is apply multiple patterns to one set of data. This can be done by finding a primary pattern and then subtracting that pattern from the actual data and then using these differences as input data for a new pattern search. So, for the example discussed earlier, one could take the lengths of the differences between the actual data and the best pattern, and use those differences as input data for a new search for a pattern.

This process could be used to find the physics of the motion of an arrow fired into the sky with the primary pattern of gravity being found first and then other patterns can be found that correspond to air resistance, friction and so on. In this way, different laws, objects and patterns can be identified which, when appropriately applied, constitute the model of the world that is created by science.

A pattern-identifying process such as this is the only way that knowledge of the world beyond our senses can be ascertained. As previously mentioned, it is a continuation of the pattern identification process that we personally use to create our pyramid of patterns and model of the world. But unlike our personal pyramid of patterns which is hidden, science and its patterns are explicit. The data can be identified as well as the templates that are tested and the final pattern that is selected.

Science also has a form of a pyramid of patterns, but it is as not as elaborate as the one used for personal cognition. Science's pyramid is not constructed through a recursive process but by the multiple pattern process described above, where one pattern is built upon the foundation of others. So, for example, the theory or patterns relating to quarks are built upon many different patterns that have been established by conducting many different experiments that constructed patterns relating to macroscopic objects, molecules, atoms and perhaps also fundamental notions of time and space. So there are patterns built upon patterns that could be said to constitute a pyramid of patterns.

This highlights another difference between science and the personal normative processing of data. Typically the normative processing of sense-data is a passive process, whereas instead science actively seeks new data to expand their theories and test the accuracy and range of their theories. Often scientists will construct instruments that can detect data that is beyond the range of our simple senses and convert it into a form that we can detect with our senses, for example, a thermometer.

In this way, our personal individual model of the world can be extended to new domains and new knowledge through the pursuit of science.

Some may be concerned by the lack of certainty in the pattern- identification process, for all that one arrives at is the best pattern and not the perfect one; or at least not one that can be shown to be perfect. But this is not a problem; as all that one needs for one's model of the world, whether personal or scientific, is sufficient accuracy to be able to interact effectively with the world. Science has demonstrated this with its technological spin-offs, which have created things like cell phones, computers and other things that would be entirely impossible without an accurate model of the scientific world. But of course, this inherent uncertainty can create paradigm shifts within science as mooted by Thomas Kuhn; where a pattern that is fairly low down within the pyramid of scientific patterns, gets replaced by a better pattern, and this can cause a ripple effect on all the other patterns that were built upon it; this would constitute a paradigm shift.

So what one ends up with is an accurate model of the world, but one for which there may forever be room for improvement. For it can never be proven that one has arrived at the best possible pattern to fit the data, all one can have is the best pattern currently available. Hence one cannot rationally claim that matter obeys the laws of physics; instead one can only claim that the laws of physics constitute an accurate description of how matter moves and interacts with other matter.

One can hardly talk about physics without talking about mathematics as well. Mathematics is an extremely useful tool for finding possible templates for the pattern-identifying process. However, as described in the previous chapter, mathematics is, in essence, an entirely abstract system. Mathematics is an abstract system for the manipulation of symbols according to specified rules. It requires a mapping from those symbols to elements within a pyramid of patterns for mathematics to have any connection to a non-abstract world. It requires a mapping between the symbols of mathematics and a measurement or data to apply it to the real world. It also requires a unit of measurement such as a second, metre or kilogram. It is only through such a mapping that mathematics can relate to the world beyond our senses.

Science is a process carried out by many different people and groups of people and some may come up with different patterns or theories, which they claim to be good patterns or good theories but which may be at odds with other people's theories. So the question is then: 'What tests can one apply to a theory to determine its efficacy?' Perhaps the best test is: 'Is the theory or pattern able to recreate the data to a sufficient degree of accuracy?' This test would be particularly effective in repudiating hand-waving pseudo-science theories which, in general, are entirely ineffectual at recreating data. A secondary test would relate to the simplicity of the theory as the simpler the theory, the greater the data compression.

The reason science has been so successful is that it has extended the basic process of pattern identification of individuals into the domain of experiments and instruments that can extend the input data beyond that of our raw senses; such as through microscopes and telescopes.

However, I would like to add some additional notes. (These notes refer specifically to physics rather than science in general.)

1 There is no requirement for a theory in physics to be compatible with the normative perceptions of personal pattern identification. So, for example, it may be necessary for the perception of time and space in physics to be quite different from normative notions.

2. No theory, no matter how strange, should be definitively ruled out as being a possible template for a pattern. For if the template doesn't fit the data, it can simply be rejected. The only requirement for a good theory is that it constitutes the best available pattern to fit the relevant data and also compresses the data such that the description of the theory requires less information than the data itself.

3. Physics creates a model of the physical world, and this model is not the same as the actual real world beyond our senses. This realisation may provide some insight into the famous Schrödinger's cat thought experiment paradox.

In quantum mechanics, the theories typically generate probabilities for possible outcomes rather than the theory fitting the actual data. Probability is an indication of ignorance of a full description of the circumstances, no matter whether it is through hidden or unknown parameters or perhaps inherent randomness, and as such the probabilities only refer to ones limited knowledge of the situation. For the probabilities do not refer to the actual real world beyond our senses, for whenever an observation is actually made, it is never of a probability but only of some fixed quantity. Probabilities are only ever inferred from statistical data. Instead, the probabilities only have meaning with regard to ones model of the world and that particular situation.

This is applicable to the Schrödinger's cat thought experiment. For it is not the situation that the actual cat is in a superposition of states of being simultaneously alive and dead, it is only one's knowledge of the situation that constitutes a superposition of the two possible outcomes. So when the box is subsequently opened it is only one's knowledge of the situation that 'collapses' into one state or the other.

4. There are also implications for the 'Many worlds' theory regarding quantum weirdness and the collapse of the wave function. One of the tests for a good pattern is that the pattern constitutes a compression of the original data, i.e. the pattern needs to be simpler than the data and the more simple it is so much the better, for a given accuracy.

The 'Many Worlds'. theory asserts that the wave does not collapse at all but that instead the world splits into different worlds with a different outcome in each world. However, as a scientific theory, this 'Many Worlds' theory fails on both the criteria mentioned earlier. Firstly, it is incapable of reproducing the data of the world we actually live in and experience; it cannot reproduce the data of where and how the wave actually collapses. Secondly, it does not constitute a compression of the data. The Many Worlds hypothesis is highly complex, with many unanswered questions such as 'What happens in the other worlds?' 'Where are they?' 'How many other worlds are there?' 'What are the exact criteria for a world to divide into many worlds?' The complexity of the theory far exceeds that of the original data. In the light of this, it would seem that the Many Worlds hypothesis is not a good scientific theory.

A good scientific theory is one that is concise and can reproduce the data efficiently. If it cannot reproduce the data then it may not be a scientific theory at all.

This venture into science shows how science is a natural extension of the pattern-identifying process used for cognition and that it has the same foundations and processes.

# Chapter 16
# Words, Language and Communication

*Our journey now takes us to the domain of communication; communication with other people where words are labels for patterns.*

In this chapter, I want to show how language and communication emerges from the foundations of the Pattern Paradigm philosophy, and through this, to get a better understanding of what language and communication are.

We have this wonderful gift of language and the communication that it makes possible. It is one that none of our distant relatives in the animal kingdom possess. It is perhaps the defining difference between humans and all other animals. It means that we can share ideas; we don't have to work out everything for ourselves; instead we can learn from other people how to do things and learn facts about the world that are beyond our immediate environment.

In this way, human knowledge, through speech and writing, can accumulates that we can learn more and more about the world. In this chapter, I'll be referring specifically to the human language of speech and writing, and I will be using the English language to communicate the ideas. So I won't be including body language, sign language and other means of communication. While other animals do communicate with each other; it is not in the form of communication that I will be talking about.

In previous chapters, It was discussed how we create a model of the world through the logical process of pattern identification from sense-data. The patterns can subsequently create a hierarchy of patterns that I call a 'pyramid of patterns'. Individual patterns can be given identifying labels.

In the higher part of the pyramid of patterns, patterns can be given labels that can be spoken as words. So that is what words are: words are labels for patterns. The essential part of language is the ability to articulate unique sounds, which represent labels for patterns in one's pyramid of patterns. Then one can achieve communication between people when there is a commonality of those sounds which represent the same or similar patterns in both their pyramid of patterns.

People learn this commonality as children by identifying an object or an action and then being told what the sound or name associated with that object or action is. The English learn that a tree is a 'tree', the French call it something else. In this way, children learn their language, and this proceeds into adulthood, with more and more words being identified with their patterns. Along with this, the child learns the grammar associated with that language, i.e. the order in which to put words and where to put prepositions and conjunctions to convey simple messages clearly and unambiguously.

An important point, with regard to the philosophy of language, is that the connection between the words and the things that they are purported to represent is a long and complex one. It is not just a simple and direct relationship between a word and what it is purported to represent. In brief, it starts with sense-data which gets processed using pattern identification logic to identify a pattern, which then gets combined with other patterns to create a model of the world. These high-level patterns are given labels which can be spoken and communicated. So there is no definitive reality for the words to get linked to. However, typically in modern parlance, this complex chain of inference is ignored and a word is taken to be a direct representation of the reality of the world beyond our senses.

So now with a shared and comprehensive vocabulary two people can communicate with each other in amazing ways, share information, not only about the world but also about their inner selves.

Communication is a two stage process; it requires a transmitter or speaker or writer at the first stage to transmit the communication and a receiver or listener or reader at the second stage to interpret the communication. So what can be communicated? Information, instructions, orders, ideas, jokes, philosophy; whatever you like. Why communicate? Well, there are many benefits of communication; and perhaps the most significant one is learning from other people about the material world and the technology that emanates from that; and subsequently teaching other people in turn. The technology we have today would be completely impossible without a comprehensive language. Also, this explosion of knowledge was hugely facilitated by the invention of writing; written words being a representation of the sound of normal speech.

But what is the essential logic behind the desire to communicate? How is the little logical processor, whose journey we have been describing, going to decide when to speak and when to remain silent?

In Chapter 12, 'The Logic of Decision-Making', an algorithm was put forward that crudely described how a decision could be made and a subsequent action effected. I will summarise it briefly here.

In essence, the logical process of decision making is one whereby all possible decisions are considered together with all their possible consequences. Then the decision that is determined to be most likely to lead to the greatest amount of happiness for oneself (or least amount of unhappiness) is selected.

Deciding to communicate and enacting that decision, falls within the general domain of decision-making; so this algorithm applies to decisions about what and when to communicate. It may seem fairly trivial to make a decision to ask someone to 'pass me a spanner', but the same logic is applicable to this action as to ask someone for a hand in marriage. It is a logical process of decision-making and an essential part of the process in that the aim or purpose of the decision is to maximise the happiness of the person (or the little logical processor) that is always, subconsciously perhaps, wanting to maximise their happiness.

Once the decision to communicate has been made the appropriate pattern for that communication can be assembled and the labels arranged in a grammatically meaningful form and then transmitted as a string of sounds or words.

The logic for the receiver of the communication as to what decision and action to take following the transmitter sending the communication is slightly more complex, as it requires a process of interpreting or translating the words of the communication, and there may be some ambiguity or uncertainty as to that interpretation. But assuming that the receiver has made some sort of sense from the communication, how is the receiver to respond, if at all, to the communication? Well, again it follows the logic of the decision-making algorithm already described; the receiver of the communication will make a decision and then effect an action based upon their model of the world and how they can maximise their happiness. This is a complex process and one that would be unique to each individual.

Broadly speaking, there would seem to be two main categories for the use of communication which it might be useful to distinguish.

1. Working with other people towards a common goal. Communication in this area would be referring to the present; 'let's do this', 'help me with that', that sort of thing.

2. Learning from other people as to how one can improve one's understanding of the world and subsequently teaching others so that they can improve theirs.

In category 1, one would get things like requests, commands and warnings. Whereas in category 2, one would get things like information possibilities, stories, jokes and opinions.

It is important to note that the receiver does not know, with certainty, what the motivation of the transmitter is; nor the details of their decision-making process. However, the receiver does have a choice in determining how to respond to the communication. The possible choices will include those that may seem to be counter-intuitive. A command does not have to be treated as a command, any more than an intended insult has to be treated as an insult.

Facts, opinions and general information do not have to be believed nor incorporated into one's pyramid of patterns, at least not without some due process of verification. Another factor that is associated with this is the question of whether the purported facts are potentially significant or merely trivial. So, for example, if someone was talking about an axe murderer being present in the district, that would be important and significant and if they're talking about a stain on the carpet, well, that's fairly trivial.

Communication is a 2-person process; there is a transmitter and a receiver; though these two people could be separated by time and space. The communications of Herodotus, for example, can still be received today. And the writer of an encyclopedia is a transmitter and the reader of the encyclopedia is a receiver. The transmitter and receiver may even be the same person separated over time, say by writing something in a diary that the person might want to recall later; it is still a communication. Language is the medium by which such communications can be effected.

In conclusion, this approach to language and communication follows smoothly and logically from the original precepts of the Pattern Paradigm philosophy; which included the supposition of a logical processor trying to interact with the world and to make sense of the world, and now, much later, to communicate with other logical processors.

As a final point, language is the medium for the practice of philosophy. Without language there would be no philosophy, one would simply have one's own ideas locked in one's head. Philosophy is about communication; the communication of ideas and of what makes sense and that which does not.

# Chapter 17
# Culture and Schisms

*Our journey now takes us to explore the impact of language and how pressure from communities can influence one's life.*

In the previous chapter, we looked at the logic of words, language and communication; and this was primarily looking at communication between two people. While language and communication have been hugely beneficial to the human race, there is also a downside to communication, and this is what I want to discuss in this chapter. Specifically, I want to look at how a young person can process information imparted to them by proponents of their culture and society.

For clarity, I will use the dictionary definition of culture, which is: 'the ideas customs and social behaviour of a particular people or society'. Social animals have a form of culture too; behaviour as to how to fit into the group is learnt; as evidenced in the social behaviour of animals such as elephants, chimpanzees and wolves. No doubt these animal cultures have evolved in order to facilitate the efficient operation and function of the group. These cultures will be learnt by imitating the actions of others within the group. They will be learnt by the youngsters, by imitating the actions of others in the group; with perhaps some form of physical retribution if a youngster strays too far from what is expected.

Human culture is somewhat different in that almost all of it is communicated and learnt through language; children are instructed on how to behave. Human culture is steeped in history and tradition. Typically, it was created long ago by people who sought particular modes of behaviour in others. The environment in which it was created, both socially and technologically, may be far different from the environment of today's societies. So the efficiency of a society's culture may have been high long ago but may not be so efficient today, but that is OK. The requirement for a culture is for it to be functional and workable; it does not have to be super efficient.

The question that I want to pose is: 'How is a child to make sense of the culture in which they are being raised? In this philosophical journey, we have been looking at how a simple logical processor with sensory inputs and motor outputs can interact effectively with the physical world; it creates a pyramid of patterns from sense-data and makes decisions to interact with the world.

So now we arrive at our little logical processor as a child within a community. It encounters the culture of the community; i.e. the ideas, customs, mores and social behaviour of that community. So how can it fit these mores into its pyramid of patterns? There is considerable social pressure to conform and accept the culture; for to shun the culture of one's society is to risk ostracism, or even expulsion from the community; whereas to accept it, is to feel safe and protected; in much the same way that a bird in the centre of a flock, or a fish in the centre of its shoal feels safe and protected.

Some aspects of human culture can be learnt from simple observations of behaviour of other people and then imitating it. It is well-known, for example, that babies like to imitate the actions of those they encounter. So imitation is a very natural thing to do. However, much of human culture is communicated to children through language. When these communications relate to how to behave in particular situations, how to dress, how to speak and so on, there is no particular problem; a child can follow the instructions and fit in with the culture and society. However, it is somewhat different when it comes to instructions on how to think; such as 'don't be selfish', 'think of others', 'believe in God', 'do as you're told'; these are ideas relating to how a child is expected to think, rather than merely how to act in specific situations.

In this regard, it impinges on their pre-existing pyramid of patterns. Then the question is: 'How are the ideas, which are contained in the communications, to be integrated into a child's pyramid of patterns?'

Normally, patterns are created from the ground up, for this is how a pyramid of patterns is created, with its foundation on basic sense-data. Then if someone who is promoting the culture of the society, communicates a particular pattern, or idea to the child, the child can use that particular idea or pattern as a template in their pattern-identifying process.

Then, so long as they have sufficient data with which to test the template, they can use that particular template within their pattern-identifying process and determine for themselves whether the suggested idea or pattern constitutes the best pattern to fit with their existing data; or if it is not quite the best pattern that it is at least an effective or efficient pattern.

If it is found that the suggested idea or pattern of the culture is effective and the best pattern, then the suggested pattern can be smoothly integrated into their pyramid of patterns. If this is the case, then the child can quite happily accept this and perhaps also all other aspects of their culture and never question nor worry about whether the ideas of their culture are, in fact, the very best patterns; they simply accept the ideas and mores for themselves and integrate smoothly into their society.

However, if the suggested idea or pattern regarding the culture does not fit smoothly and seamlessly into their pyramid of patterns, then this can create problems. If this is the case, there are two main options for the child:

1. They can reject the suggested cultural idea and instead adopt a pattern that is better suited to their patterns and data available to them. I.e. they just create their own best pattern from the relevant data.

Or 2. They can adopt the suggested cultural idea or pattern, while recognising at the same time that it does not fit smoothly into their pyramid of patterns.

However, there are problems with both options. The problem with rejecting the suggested pattern and adopting one of the child's own creations is that it is putting itself at odds with the mainstream culture of their society. The problem with option 2 is that if the child accepts the suggested pattern, even though it does not fit well with their pyramid of patterns, it can create a discontinuity or schism in the child's pyramid of patterns.

A visual representation of this schism might look like what is called the Trident Impossibility: the base of the diagram looks fine, and it is easy to see it as a 3D image.

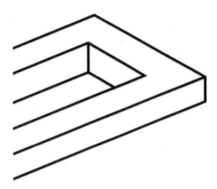

Similarly, with the other end of the diagram, it too is easy to see as a 3D image.

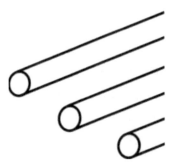

However, in putting the two together, there is a discontinuity in the 3D image, even though the lines seem to connect. It cannot be seen in its totality as a 3D image; there is a schism in the centre.

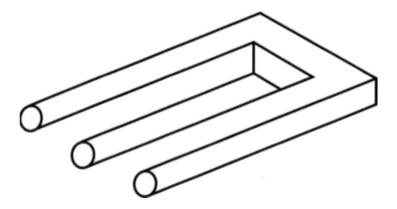

Of course, every child is different and the specific culture in which they are raised is also different from that of others. Some children have no difficulty in accepting the culture of their society together with their morals and mores; they can become well integrated into their society.

Other children will reject the mores of their society, and they will encounter problems; they're likely to be termed as 'troublemakers' or 'out of control'. Their lives will be hard as they struggle to make sense of the culture in which they find themselves and to find a place for themselves within their society.

But it is perhaps a third group: those who reluctantly accept the mores of their culture but find that they are afflicted with schisms in their pyramid of patterns, that I want to focus on.

The culture of a society, by its very nature, extols the merits of the group and doing things for the group. In so doing, it minimises and suppresses the merits of individualism and the individual. This suppression can cause schisms in the pyramid of patterns of an individual child, as previously discussed. And these schisms can cause disharmony in a person's pyramid of patterns and a general feeling of ill ease or even alienation. These schisms can also cause problems in their process of decision-making.

For when accessing a pattern that has a schism there are two possibilities, one relating to the deeper pattern and one relating to society's culture. It is akin to measuring a distance and finding that it has two disparate values, such as 0.5 kilometres and 38 kilometres and having to decide whether to walk or take a bus. This can cause difficulty in reaching good decisions and which can, in turn, cause stress. There is no easy remedy, short of delving deep into the foundations of one's pyramid of patterns and also delving deep into the foundations of the mores of culture and society. Neither of which are viable strategies for a child or youngster with their limited knowledge and experience of both themselves and the world.

Some proponents of the culture might naively claim that such schisms are simply the price one has to pay for living in a complex human society and that youth should simply accept the precepts and mores of society and learn to live with the schisms or perhaps just ignore them.

However, it must be remembered that the mores are not necessarily an efficient way of interacting with society. They have been cobbled together over time and may in fact be highly inaccurate and so if a youth believes these mores to be accurate and unquestionable, i.e. they simply adopt them in their entirety; they may find that they have a distorted or inaccurate model of the world, which can cause problems in interacting with the world.

So much so, that it may be the case that the schisms and the distortion of youth's model of the world is a major underlying cause of youth alienation and possibly also youth suicide; which is a common affliction in many countries.

(On a personal note, I first encountered these schisms at the age of 10, when they became manifest in the form of recurring, disturbing dreams in which things did not make sense and could not be resolved. (Sleep is the time when the brain, free from raw sense-data inputs, creates patterns of patterns and sorts out its pyramid of patterns.) Later on, when I was 16, one of my best friends died by suicide. It was then that I became aware of the dangers of believing cultural mores that are highly inaccurate. It was perhaps these two events that set me on the journey of exploring and investigating philosophy.)

This is a real problem in the modern world, yet it is one that is ignored by other philosophies whether religious or SWP. Indeed, it could be said that they are part of the problem; for instead of exploring ideas about individual freedom, they only put forward the case for cultural mores with their 'social contracts', 'duty' and 'moral truths'.

It is perhaps the discontinuity between what is best for the individual and what is claimed as being best for society that lies at the heart of one of the great dichotomies of philosophy.

In this book I describe the journey of the individual from its simplest origins to its place in the modern world. Its aim in this is to make sense of the modern world, an understanding that is free of schisms.

There is no necessity for discontinuities between what is best for the individual and what is best for society. While we are all individuals and thinking takes place within an individual brain, we are also social animals and gain great benefit from communicating with and learning from others.

# Chapter 18
# Disembodied Statements Are Meaningless

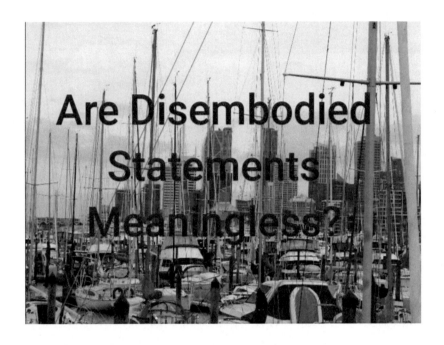

*Our journey now takes us to a blind canyon, which should be entertaining so long as we can find our way back.*

This chapter is somewhat different from the others, in that it is a brief detour in our philosophical journey, as we explore a philosophical blind canyon; one which, while popular in Standard Western Philosophy, goes nowhere and achieves nothing. Not every idea in philosophy is necessarily a productive line of enquiry. For example, the idea that the Sun goes around the Earth was popular a few hundred years ago. It may have seemed sensible at the time, but it is not a productive line of inquiry and is now generally rejected.

Specifically we shall be exploring the popular ideas that truth can be encapsulated in statements and that logic can be applied directly to words and objects. It is because of the popularity of this blind canyon and its unquestioned acceptance by so many, that we shall be exploring it. In the previous two chapters, we looked at language and culture. In those chapters, it was shown how words are labels for patterns and are used for the communication of ideas.

There is a chain of logical ideas that links words to reality, but it is a complex one.

The relationship is perhaps best shown in this diagram. It shows the linkage between the world beyond our senses and words.

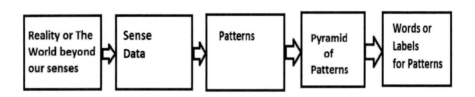

I will go over it very briefly. The world beyond our senses creates data, which are detected by our senses and from which we use pattern identification logic to identify patterns within the data. These identified patterns can then be used as input to the pattern-identifying logic in a recursive manner to create higher-level patterns. These can then be arranged in a pyramid of patterns. These patterns can then be labelled and communicated to other people using those labels or 'words'.

Everyone's identified patterns will be slightly different from everyone else's and will depend upon their personal thought processes as well as on their personal experiences. So the labels or words used in communication will indicate slightly different patterns in different people. So, for example, the word 'pink' will indicate a slightly different range of colours for different people; and there is no problem with this.

But problems have arisen when Standard Western Philosophy has ignored this complex chain that links reality to words; and instead has implicitly claimed that there is a direct and unambiguous link between words and reality as shown in this diagram.

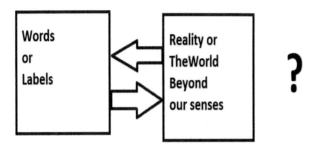

Standard Western Philosophy does this by failing to understand the necessary logical steps from sense-data to a pyramid of patterns and instead naively claims that there is a direct link between words and reality.

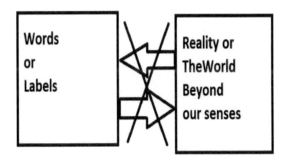

They claim that words have intrinsic meaning all on their own. But words are labels for patterns and if this link is removed, then the words are inherently meaningless and only exist as strings of alphanumeric symbols. So, for example, the word 'pink' when linked to a person with a pyramid of patterns has the meaning of a colour that one might see in a rose or fine sunset, but when removed from a connection with people, it only exists as a string of alphanumeric symbols: 'p', 'i', 'n', 'k', or perhaps as a particular sound: 'pink'. But Standard Western Philosophy naively assumes that there is a direct connection between words and what they are purported to represent; however, this is logically indefensible.

Having made this naive direct connection between words and reality, they compound this error by concocting arrangements of words in what are called 'statements' and they give those statements properties and claim that these statements can be labelled as 'true' or 'false'. But since the statements are not communications from one person to another and are removed from any person with a pyramid of patterns, they are inherently meaningless. I am referring to them as 'disembodied statements', so as to distinguish them from statements that are made by a person as a communication.

Examples of disembodied statements could include:

'This statement is true',

'This statement is false',

'Either A or not-A is true'.

'Socrates is a man, all men are mortal; hence Socrates is mortal'.

'All swans are white'.


Perhaps disembodied statements are best epitomised by the claim that statements can have truth values of 'true' or 'false' and also their so-called 'laws of logic' and 'Either p or not-p is 'true''.

A few points to note:

1. If the statements are actually communicated by a person, then they do not qualify as disembodied statements. So, for example, someone might say to you: 'This statement is false', and while not a disembodied statement, it clearly does not make any sense. Or if someone says: 'All swans are white'; this would only make sense in the context of a discussion on aquatic birds.

2. Even if the statement 'Either A or not A is true' is made as a communication, this would say nothing at all about the world. So, for example, if I were to say: 'either this rose is pink or it is not-pink', that says absolutely nothing about the world and nothing about whether the rose is pink or not.

It would only begin to say something about the world if one had an explicit process for determining whether it is 'A' or is 'not-A', or whether the rose is 'pink' or is 'not-pink'. However, there is no explicit process for determining this without involving subjective and hidden pattern identification. So, without an explicit process, all one is left with are hand-waving and entirely subjective arguments.

If somehow, disembodied statements and their property of truth could be established as an objective certainty upon which all knowledge could be linked, then this would be some achievement. But it is a logical impossibility. All the claims of truth for disembodied statements only exist in a fantasy world that has no links to the real world in which we live.

3. When disembodied statements are treated as strings of symbols, they <u>can</u> have significance, but only if they can be incorporated into a well-defined abstract system such as mathematics.

So, for example, the disembodied mathematical statement: '2+2=4' can be treated as a string of symbols. Given the particular symbols that are used, it can be associated with the system of mathematics and then identified as a theorem within the system of mathematics. Hence, it can be labelled as 'true', but only within the system of mathematics.

However, there is no abstract logical system with axioms and explicit rules of inference that uses only alphanumeric symbols. Hence the string of alphanumerical symbols: 'elephants are pink' cannot be associated with any specific logical abstract system because there is no logical abstract system that can process those particular alphanumeric symbols.

Logic needs to be rigorous if it is to be useful. It is no use having a pseudo-logical system that is rife with exceptions. So it may seem 'logical' that if 'The cat is on the mat' that it follows that 'The mat is under the cat'. While this may seem to be reasonable, this manipulation of words is not sensible when applied to 'Mrs A is on drugs'; for 'Drugs are under Mrs A' makes no sense. The 'logic' when it appears to work is no more than 'hand-waving. The popular claim that 'There are no married bachelors' is negated when one learns that Mrs A is a member of the band 'the bachelors', for then it follows that 'Mrs A is a bachelor'.

One might be able to put exceptions into the logic of the system in order to make it rigorous, but this would be extremely messy and inefficient as they would have to be many exceptions that would need to be specified and even then one could not be sure that one has identified and specified all possible exceptions. (This would not have the simplicity of the exception discussed in Chapter 14 where we saw how division by zero was excluded from mathematical operations.)

Since disembodied statements are not communications and have no identifiable origin, they can be treated as entirely random strings of words or alphanumeric symbols. For all one knows, they could have been written by a monkey with a typewriter. What was written may be of interest to a reader, or it may not. By 'interesting', I mean: 'has the possibility to be incorporated into a person's personal pyramid of patterns to create a new pattern'.

However, despite these logical problems, disembodied statements with their presumed properties of 'truth' and 'falsity' have become embedded at the heart of Standard Western Philosophy. They have done so without any explicit justification, or even rationality. In this way, Standard Western Philosophy has found itself up a blind canyon.

In the absence of such justification, it may be instructive for us to look at how it might possibly have occurred. Suppose there was a philosopher, let's call him 'Phil', who lived some while ago and who had no knowledge of the logic of the chain of links from sense-data to words. All Phil knows is that he has what he considers to be knowledge of the world and that his knowledge can be described in words. Phil also considers that what he knows is certain or indubitable, for he does not consider that there might be alternatives and so he claims that his knowledge is 'true'.

And since he can describe his knowledge in words and statements, he considers that those statements, independent from himself, can be labelled as 'true'. If statements do not fit with his knowledge of the world he labels them as 'false'. He feels justified in doing this, as other people, including other philosophers, agree with him.

In this way, the notion that disembodied statements can describe the world and be labelled as 'true', could be created. However, it is based upon the naive and inaccurate assumption that words are linked directly to things in the real world, the world beyond our senses. However, as we have seen, the connection between the two is a long and complex chain of links and is inherently subjective. Even without knowledge of this chain of links, it is philosophically naive to presume that the connection is direct and simple. The naivety that I'm referring to is akin to seeing the Sun rise in the east and set in the west and then presuming that the Sun goes around the Earth and then to believe that it is 'true' that the Sun goes around the Earth; solely for the naive reason that one is unable to envisage any alternative.

In the same way, that certainty in the belief that the Sun goes around Earth is a barrier to understanding the dynamics of the solar system, so too, a certainty that words link directly to the real world is a barrier to understanding the dynamics of knowledge and how it is created. They are both naive assumptions that are based upon the unjustified presumption that what one knows is certain and indubitable.

That said, they both also have a place in the non-philosophical normative world, where they are both functional in that the idea that the Sun goes around the Earth is fine for non-astronomers and the idea that words link directly to the real world is fine for non-philosophers.

However, from a more rigorous perspective, whether philosophical or scientific, a good theory needs to fit the facts, be useful and provide insights into the nature of the world. The theory that disembodied statements can embody truth fails on all these criteria; for there are no facts that it fits, it is not shown to be useful and neither has it generated any insights into the nature of the world.

Instead, what it has done is to distort people's view of the nature of the world and of philosophy. And what is more, it has created various logical paradoxes, such as that of the heap, Ship of Theseus and many others.

In the light of this it is clear that the idea of disembodied statements as having the property of truth goes nowhere except up a blind canyon. It has no place in proper philosophy, except perhaps in the history of philosophy as a failed exploration of ideas. For while the apparent certainty of disembodied statements might seem attractive, it is simply an illusion; the apparent certainty only exists in a fictional world.

*This concludes our brief venture into the blind canyon of disembodied statements. We can now resume our journey to more fruitful realms.*

# Chapter 19
# Is Morality a Good Ethical System?

*We now venture into the domain of ethics and explore the underlying logic of decision-making.*

Perhaps the two most important logical processes conducted by the brain are those of constructing a model of the world and that of using the model to make decisions to interact with the world.

The logic of constructing a model of the world has been described and discussed in previous chapters, specifically Chapters 8 and 9 in which an algorithm was presented to show the explicit logic of this process.

The essential logic of decision-making was discussed in Chapter 12, where another algorithm was presented to show explicitly the logic of the decision-making process. In this chapter, I want to discuss some of the Implications and limitations of the process.

Very briefly, the process requires assembling all the relevant data of the situation that requires a decision, and then each possible course of action is considered in turn. Then for each possible action, one considers the likely consequences of that action and how it is likely to influence one's personal happiness. Then one selects the action that is most likely to maximise one's happiness. This then constitutes one's decision.

However, this is a somewhat idealised description of the process. In practical terms, there are limitations to it.

Here are some implications, limitations and notes on the process:

1. One's model of the world is not perfect. There may be considerable gaps or unknowns that are relevant. Projections into the future to evaluate the possible consequences are somewhat haphazard at best. This is especially problematic when considering the consequences that one's action has on other people and how they may respond to it, as these are extremely hard to predict

2. There are often time constraints in making decisions, in fact there almost always are. From the situation of a threatening tiger to deciding whether to take a position of employment, there are time restrictions where it is expedient to make a decision rapidly.

The decision-making process is a complex one with several logical loops, where each possible consequence of every possible action needs to be identified and evaluated with regard to the likelihood of the person achieving happiness in both the short term and the long term. In fact, as the algorithm is described, it could be an endless process and typically it is only time constraints that effect the termination of the process.

3. It is not always obvious what will bring one happiness. Everyone is unique and will have a slightly different formulation of what brings them happiness (in the same way that everybody's body is slightly different from those of others).

Incidentally, I am using the word 'happiness' as the label for: 'that to which the brain aspires', which may be slightly different from the popular interpretation of the word. But there is sufficient similarity between the two to justify the use of the word in the context of decision-making.

So one needs to determine for oneself what brings one happiness in order to make effective decisions.

4. The complexity of the decision-making process may make it expedient to use some form of shortcut to simplify and speed up the process. These might

include things like: 'don't take risks', 'don't do any harm to other people', 'do what other people do', and 'stay safe'.

Many of these epithets come from other people or are a part of a person's culture.

They can be used to shortcut the decision-making process so that if an epithet that one holds becomes relevant then one can immediately accept or reject the possible action without going through all the possible consequences in detail.

5. In many cultures there is an emphasis on morals rather than on the decision-making process for describing actions and behaviour. While morals can be used as epithets to simplify the decision-making process, they are not, as some like to believe, absolute and rigid criteria for decision-making. Morals are only a guide to acceptable social behaviour.

According to the dictionary morals are those notions that are concerned with the principles of 'right' and 'wrong' behaviour. But without any explicit process for determining what is 'right' or 'wrong' (and there is none) then any such arguments for morality cannot be anything more than hand-waving.

There is a danger in posing morals as absolutes for guiding the behaviour of people as they can fail those who are most in need of guidance. For if someone with a leaning towards anti-social behaviour rejects all consideration of morals (which is easy to do), then they are left with no effective guide towards making good decisions and hence can make inefficient decisions that only have short term benefits but which are to the detriment of their long-term happiness.

Morals were created by people who had their own motivation of maximising their own personal happiness, and hence, there are no grounds for holding them as absolutes. These are sufficient reasons for rejecting morality as an effective ethical system.

Moralists would do better to point out to other people the advantages or disadvantages of the consequences of actions on the personal happiness of those people rather than merely claiming that one 'should' or 'should not' do those actions because they are 'right' or 'wrong' or 'moral' or 'immoral'.

Claiming that actions are 'right' or 'wrong' or 'good' or 'bad' merely applies a degree of social pressure and can easily be dismissed by another person, whereas evidence that a particular action will lead to specific beneficial or adverse consequences to the happiness of the person is not so easily dismissed.

6. It should be noted that laws are quite distinct from morals as they are written down explicitly and are an important part of the state legislature. The

consequences of the transgression of laws are also explicitly stated. While there is no certainty that a transgression of the laws will necessarily lead to retribution, the estimated probability that this will occur and the associated unhappiness can be factored into the decision-making process.

7. The decision-making process applies to all decisions of the brain from the most trivial to the most momentous from whether to have another slice of cake or choosing whom to marry.

These decisions apply not only to what people do but also to what they say. What people say and do has the motivation to maximise their personal happiness. The understanding of this can be useful for interpreting the motivation behind people's actions even if they claim they are doing them for entirely altruistic reasons.

8. Humans are unique among animals in having knowledge of how long that they can expect to live. As such, more than other animals, people can make consideration for the long-term consequences of their actions (even to future generations), and so can make decisions that will benefit their long-term happiness and be less concerned about their short-term happiness.

Incidentally, many animals do consider their long-term happiness though this is typically only over the period of a year and may in fact be more instinctive than rational. So animals such as squirrels can put away a food store for the winter. Other animals migrate to seasonal feeding grounds or breeding grounds, such as godwits, seals and wildebeests.

So how can one maximise the efficiency of one's decision-making?

Here are some suggestions:

1.  Learn about the world, especially one's immediate environment and the people within it so as to create a good model of the world.
2.  Take time to review the outcomes of one's decisions so that one can improve one's decision-making for similar situations in the future.
3.  Take note of what actually makes one happy and make decisions that will maximise one's happiness in the long term.
4.  Avoid taking actions for which the outcome is highly uncertain and possibly injurious such as breaking things, harming other people or telling lies.
5.  Be guided by other people's epithets and codes of conduct.

## Conclusion

The decision-making process is not an easy one; there Is always a lack of certainty in predicting the outcome. Making decisions to find happiness in either the short term or the long term is not a certainty, but that is life. We have large brains and a model of the world so that we can make good decisions. We have no option but to make decisions in the best way that we can. Morals can be considered to be guidelines, but nothing more.

# Chapter 20
# What Is Truth?

# What is Truth?

*We now venture into the domain of 'truth'; for many, it is the elusive holy grail of philosophy, but is it? Let us explore.*

So what is truth?

According to the Pattern Paradigm, words are labels for patterns; 'truth' is a word, and hence, it is a label for a pattern. But for what pattern is it a label?

According to the dictionary, 'truth' is: 'That which is in accordance with fact or reality'. This is fine for normal everyday communication, but from a rigorous philosophical perspective, there is the rather large problem of: How is it determined whether something is in accordance with fact or reality?

In the normative world this problem is ignored and instead the word 'truth' is used as having the same meaning as 'certainty'. If someone claims that something is 'true', their claim is equivalent to claiming that it is 'certain'.

So what is certain? How can certainty be found?

Abstract systems, such as mathematics, would seem to be an obvious place to start. These systems were discussed in Chapter 13. Abstract systems have symbols, rules, axioms and theorems; however, they have no direct link to sense-data. Hence they are not a part of the real world and are abstract. Abstract systems are entirely self-sufficient and isolated from reality.

It is not hard to create an abstract system. So let us consider a fairly trivial example:

**Name:** Mathematics (Subset)
**Axioms:** '1+1=2', '1+1+1+1=4'
**Rules:**'1+1' may be substituted for '2'
**Theorem:** '2+2=4' (by the second axiom and the rules)

The theorem follows explicitly from the rules and axioms of the system. Therefore it cannot be doubted; it is certain. Hence the theorem '2+2=4' can be considered to be true, albeit only within that particular abstract system.

Or to take another example of a trivial abstract logical system:

**Name:** Alpha
**Axioms:** 'ABC'
**Rule:** The string 'AB' may be substituted for the string 'BA'.
**Theorem:** 'BAC' (by the axiom and the rule)

The theorem 'BAC' can then be said to be 'true' within the system of Alpha.

These examples demonstrate the use of the word 'true' when applied to abstract logical systems. This label of 'true' may be useful to distinguish theorems of the system from non-theorems of the system. So the string of symbols '2+2=4' is a theorem of mathematics and can be labelled as 'true'; whereas the string '2+2=5' is not a theorem of the system and can be labelled as 'false' within the system of mathematics.

This brings us to the concept of truth as applied to a person's model of the world. Knowledge of the world can only be created from sense-data, as our senses are the only link between the exterior world and the mind.

But how is knowledge extracted from sense-data? It is not a magical process, but rather a logical process. I have discussed this in some detail in Chapter 8 'Patterns, Time and Space' and Chapter 9 'Pyramids, Patterns and Why We Sleep'.

While the logical process is rigorous and can be described by an algorithm, it is not strictly deductive. For given some particular sense-data as input, the output theorem (which is the identified pattern) is not strictly determined. It can depend upon the variation of the templates that are tested and the amount of time given to the process. (The process ends when one runs out of templates to test or runs out of time to devote to processing.)

Having found one's best pattern for a particular set of data, there is no certainty that a better pattern could not be found. So should one have more data, a greater imagination and unlimited time, one might be able to find a better pattern. Nevertheless, it may be pragmatic, to label the best pattern that one has found as 'certain'. This is because one's pyramid of patterns requires stability. When using lower-level patterns to create higher-level ones, the lower-level ones need to be assumed to be certain in order to create a stable pyramid of patterns. This stability is important when one uses one's pyramid of patterns as a basis for decision-making, especially if decisions need to be made rapidly.

So, for example, if a crude interpretation of some new sense-data indicates that a tiger is about to leap towards oneself, one doesn't want to waste time checking on one's interpretation of the light and shadows around the tiger or of whether it is actually a tiger rather than, say, a leopard; nor whether it is actually oneself in front of the tiger rather than, say, a virtual reality interpretation of oneself. No, the pragmatic logic is to presume that one's perception is accurate and that it _is_ a tiger and that it _is_ oneself in front of the tiger and then to remove oneself very rapidly from the vicinity of the tiger. In other words, there is a pragmatic benefit in presuming that one's best patterns of the world are accurate and certain.

Since these patterns are created in an individual person's mind, it is from a subjective perspective that one's beliefs are labelled as 'certain'. However, from a more objective and philosophical perspective and because of the nature of the pattern identification algorithm, no pattern that is created from sense-data, which includes all the patterns that refer to what we call the real world, can be definitively claimed to be certain or true; for one can never be sure that there is not some hitherto undiscovered pattern that is an improvement upon any of the patterns that anyone currently holds. That said, some patterns are undoubtedly a more accurate fit to the data than others and hence are less likely, at least within one's own lifetime, to be improved upon than others.

So, for example, the patterns that one uses to interpret raw visual data and convert that data into a 3D picture of the world are well established from large amounts of data and are confirmed by correlating them with patterns from other sense-data, such as sound, touch and smell. In contrast, the notion that the Sun goes around the Earth, which was a commonly held belief up to a few hundred years ago, was based upon a limited amount of sense-data. It was later that Galileo, using his telescope, found some additional data that did not fit with the notion that the Sun goes around the Earth. So he proposed the now well-accepted theory that it is, in fact, the Earth that orbits the Sun and not the other way around (and also that the Earth spins on its axis). However, up to that time, the idea that the Sun orbits the Earth was believed and held to be 'true'.

We have discussed the two main categories of truth: the one that applies to abstract logical systems and is explicit and overt and can be said to be objective and the other which is based on pattern identification and applies to one's model of the world and is pragmatic, yet it is hidden and subjective. It is subjective because the processes of the mind are hidden and personal; no other person can know the details of the logic that was used to arrive at a particular best pattern by a particular person. It should perhaps be noted, that while almost everyone might arrive at the same particular pattern, e.g. 'trees are made of wood', this would constitute no more than a consensus of subjective beliefs or 'truth' and would not constitute an objective 'truth'.

Everyone has a model of the world, and it is a subjective model; there is no direct logical link to an external world. The only link between them is sense-data. Nevertheless, if a person is considered to be giving an honest and accurate representation of what they believe, they can be said to be telling the truth; this is in contrast to the situation where it is considered that the person is not giving an honest and accurate representation of what they believe and hence can be said to be 'lying'.

Truth is equivalent to certainty; and people like certainty, for certainty is simple; whereas uncertainty is complex. And as mentioned, there are pragmatic benefits to certainty. But certainty is also a barrier to learning; for if one believes that something is certain then one is not going to re-examine that something at a later time to confirm whether it is still the best pattern to fit the available data.

Certainty is the subjective conviction that there is no possible alternative. So to achieve this subjective conviction it is useful to have a limited amount of data, a limited amount of time to process the data and a limited imagination. This is analogous to a starfish that lives its life in a rock pool. From the perspective of the starfish, its rock pool is the entire universe and nothing exists beyond it, and this is certain, true and indubitable. So, given this analogy, certainty and truth are not necessarily things to aspire to, and claims of truth and certainty may justifiably be treated with a certain amount of scepticism.

In common parlance, it is typically taken that words refer directly to the things they are purported to represent; so when people talk about a 'brick' or a 'tree', they presume that they are referring to a real actual brick or a real actual tree, what some might call the 'noumena'. This is fine for everyday conversation, but our only connection to some hypothesised real world is through sense-data. (The idea of a real world existing beyond our senses is a high-level pattern in the pyramid of patterns that is ultimately created from sense-data.)

The logical connection between a word such as 'brick' or 'tree' and the hypothesised actual existence of a brick or tree is a very long and complex one. The idea that there is a simple direct link between the two does not withstand rigorous philosophical scrutiny.

Despite this, there is an idea, which is popular in Standard Western philosophy, that disembodied statements, i.e. statements that exist independent of a communicator, can refer to the real world independently of the mind. This is philosophically naive. The popular claim that such statements can be 'true' or 'false' is very naive.

The only disembodied statements that can be said to be rigorously true, do not refer to any real world or model of the world but instead reside solely within logical abstract systems such as mathematics. For example, '2+2=4' or even '2y+2y = 4y' can be claimed as being 'true' within the system of mathematics. (Although these statements are in Mathematical notation, they can still be regarded as disembodied statements.) It can only be claimed that these 'statements' are 'true within the system of mathematics', they cannot be extrapolated directly to the real world.

Statements such as '2 sheep + 2 sheep = 4 sheep' require a subjective mapping process, which maps symbols of the system of mathematics onto words or concepts within a person's model of the world, such as sheep. This mapping process is not logically rigorous but is a matter of trial and error in order to determine which part of mathematics, if any, is useful in making sense of and understanding the world. (This was discussed in Chapter 14.)

So, for example, it requires trial and error to determine which of the mathematical processes of arithmetic, calculus or complex numbers is useful for understanding sheep in a field, the motion of heavenly bodies or electrodynamics. Hence this requirement for a trial-and-error mapping negates the certainty that exists within the abstract system of pure mathematics. Real-world patterns, such as 'sheep' are highly complex, hence they cannot be incorporated as simple elements into a rigorous and logical system such as that of mathematics.

The only way that words can be incorporated into an abstract system is if they are treated as simple strings of alphanumeric characters. Such an abstract system could incorporate into its rules all the rules of grammar and also incorporate into its axioms the complete contents of a dictionary. In this way, it could generate theorems of the form: 'all elephants are mammals'. However, it would be treating the words solely as strings of alphanumeric characters, it would have no concept of what an elephant or mammal actually was in reality.

If the abstract system was sufficiently comprehensive it could include, within its axioms, the entire contents of an encyclopedia and other written sources of information. This is, in effect, what modern artificial intelligence systems, such as ChatGPT, have done. The theorems it generates could be said to be certain or even 'true' within its particular abstract system. Nevertheless, its theorems are best considered as disembodied statements, they have no meaning unless or until they are interpreted by a human with a pyramid of patterns that can then map the theorems to the real world.

Even if such artificial intelligence was linked to senses and motor outputs it would still be no more than a mechanical machine in the same way that a dishwasher is a mechanical machine; for it would have no model of the world, no pyramid of patterns and no concept of reality.

Whether a form of artificial intelligence could ever be programmed so that it could identify patterns of perception and create for itself a pyramid of patterns, and hence, a model of the world is a moot point. Whether anyone would want to try to achieve this is another moot point. In any case, such an attempt would be far in the future.

Incidentally, ChatGPT is entirely bereft of a sense of humour and the ability to create jokes, this is because it has no pyramid of patterns and no concept of reality. (A pyramid of patterns is a first requirement for creating and appreciating humour and jokes.)

So to summarise, 'truth' is a label for certainty. The axioms and theorems of an abstract system can be said to be 'true' within their particular system, and they can also be said to be objective as they are essentially independent of the mind. And with regard to one's model of the world, a pattern that has been created from sense-data that is highly accurate, highly simple and has been created from a multitude of data with much processing time and imagination can be claimed to be the best available pattern to fit the relevant data and so, can be given the label 'true'.

Nevertheless, it is a subjective pattern as it requires a mind to do the processing; and it can never be proven that such a pattern is the best possible pattern to fit the data. The label of 'truth' that we typically apply to knowledge of the world is purely a pragmatic one. Often the word 'true' is used as a word of propaganda whereby the statement 'this is true' really means: 'I claim that this is certain, and I want you to believe it is certain too'.

It may also be noted that throughout this book, I rarely use the word 'true', except of course in this chapter, for there is no need for it.

# Chapter 21
# How Well Does the Pattern Paradigm Stack Up as a Philosophy?

*We now take a look back at how far we have come in our journey and evaluate what, if anything, we have achieved.*

In this chapter, I want to take a pause from developing the ideas of The Pattern Paradigm and instead take stock of how far we have come and how well The Pattern Paradigm stacks up as a philosophical paradigm. When we've done this, we can compare it with the score I gave to Standard Western Philosophy, back in Chapter 5 'How Does Standard Western Philosophy Stack Up as a Philosophical Paradigm?'

Before we get into that, I want to give a bit of background. The Pattern Paradigm is a new and original philosophical paradigm and one might ask, why is there a need for a new philosophical paradigm?

I started my explorations of philosophy following the disquiet I felt with the philosophies I encountered in childhood and early adulthood. I grew up in a society where Christianity and Standard Western Philosophy were the predominant philosophies, but I liked neither. I couldn't accept the precepts of neither Christianity nor Standard Western Philosophy, they just seemed to be a banal combination of irrelevance and 'moral truths' that were neither moral nor true. They didn't make sense.

Like so many other young people at the time who sought answers with deeper meaning, I sought something better. But rather than look to Eastern philosophies for answers or resign myself to living in a philosophical vacuum, I decided to explore the world of knowledge and seek answers for myself. To cut a long story short, I eventually arrived at the Pattern Paradigm; the philosophy that I've been describing in this book.

Perhaps the deepest question that I sought to answer and one that nobody else seemed to be asking was: How is it possible to create a model of the world from nothing more than a logical processor and sense-data?

The answer that I arrived at, as being the only possible logical process was one of pattern identification; searching for patterns within the data and building on them. Since this is so fundamental to my philosophy, I named the philosophy 'The Pattern Paradigm'.

To emphasise the logic of this process, I devised a pattern-identifying algorithm to describe how this process can work. (See Chapter 8 'Patterns, Time and Space' for details of this.) The identified patterns can only become useful if they are used to make decisions to enhance one's interactions with the external world and to enhance one's own personal well-being. To show how the logic of this can work, I devised a decision-making algorithm. (This algorithm is described in Chapter 12 'The Logic of Decision-Making'.) These two algorithms lie at the heart of the Pattern Paradigm philosophy.

It was also realised at an early stage that the logic of mathematics and other abstract systems (systems that have no direct connection to sense-data) was quite different. Their logic is based on symbols, axioms and rules which are used to generate theorems. (See Chapter 14 'The Foundations of Mathematics' for further details.)

With these philosophical foundations, the ideas were extrapolated to science, language and ethics to create a fairly comprehensive, yet simple and logical philosophy. While this is by no means the end of this philosophical journey, it is a place to take stock and see how far we have come.

Most of the main ideas have been presented; the hard work has been done. The skeleton of the ideas has been presented and fitted together into a cohesive whole. From here on, it is mostly a matter of seeing where these ideas take us and fleshing out the skeleton.

When I first got the idea of presenting this philosophy, I realised that I needed to compare The Pattern Paradigm with Standard Western Philosophy as a competing philosophical paradigm, so I would need some criteria for comparing disparate philosophical paradigms.

So what are the criteria by which philosophical paradigms can be compared and evaluated? This was another question that nobody seemed to have asked before. And the six criteria that I came up with were: Self-consistency, Comprehensiveness, Accuracy, Logic, Explicitness and Simplicity; which can be combined into the acronym SCALES. (I discussed this in Chapter 4 'What Makes for a Good Philosophical Paradigm?')

So let us move on to evaluating The Pattern Paradigm according to these criteria.

### 1. *Self-consistency*

A philosophical paradigm needs to be a cohesive whole with continuity and clear links between the various different domains. The Pattern Paradigm satisfies this in that, as I have described in this journey, there are clear links and cohesiveness between the various ideas, and there is no contradiction from one end to the next. So I give the pattern paradigm a score of 8 out of 10 for self-consistency.

### 2. *Comprehensiveness*

A philosophical paradigm needs to cover all the significant domains of life. The Pattern Paradigm satisfies this as it covers all the main domains from epistemology, mathematics and science, to decision-making and ethics. It also covers meta-philosophy in its discussion of the comparison of philosophical paradigms and SCALES. It even covers the fundamental separation of mind from matter. (This was discussed in Chapter 7 'The Deepest Depths of Philosophy'.)

However, so far, it only describes the bare skeleton of ideas and needs some filling in of the details. So I'm giving it 5 out of 10 for comprehensiveness.

### 3. *Accuracy*

A philosophical paradigm needs to describe the world as we experience it; as opposed to describing some unreal or fantasy world. The Pattern Paradigm achieves this as it is closely aligned with how knowledge is achieved and how that knowledge can be put to practical use. It even has theories for why we sleep and a theory of consciousness; neither of which were directly sought but instead emerged from the underlying basic theories.

So I am giving The Pattern Paradigm 8 out of 10 for accuracy.

### 4. *Logic*

Now we come to logic: logic is all about the fine details of how inferences are made. Logic is important for any philosophical paradigm in order to show how the ideas are linked together in an explicit and logical way; as opposed to mere hand-waving arguments. The Pattern Paradigm achieves this by providing explicit logical algorithms for perception (the pattern identification algorithm), for decision-making (the decision-making algorithm) and a logical description for the foundation of abstract systems such as mathematics.

So I give The Pattern Paradigm 8 out of 10 for logic.

### 5. *Explicitness*

Now, we come to explicitness. It is essential for a philosophical paradigm to be explicit with regard to its foundational assumptions and the logical processes by which inferences are made. The Pattern Paradigm explicitly describes its foundations in Chapters 6: 'Preparation for a philosophical journey' and 8: 'Patterns, time and space'. It also explicitly describes its logical processes in the algorithms mentioned in the previous section.

So I give The Pattern Paradigm 9 out of 10 for explicitness.

### 6. *Simplicity*

The last criterion is simplicity. It is important for a philosophical paradigm to be simple and not get lost in long convoluted arguments using obscure and possibly meaningless words. The Pattern Paradigm achieves this by being described in a clear, simple and logical language. That said, there is always room for improvement.

So I give it a score of 7 out of 10 for simplicity.

*Total score*

Totting up the scores of 8, 5, 8, 8, 9 and 7 for the six criteria of SCALES, this comes to a total of 45 out of a possible 60, for an average of 7½ out of 10. So overall, I am giving The Pattern Paradigm a score of 7½/10.

This compares with a score of 3½/10, which I gave to Standard Western Philosophy in Chapter 5. So this gives me some justification for my claim that The Pattern Paradigm is the best philosophical paradigm currently available.

# Chapter 22
# Eleven Uses of a Good Philosophy

*In this part of the journey, we delve into the practical applications that may be possible from a good theoretical philosophy such as the Pattern Paradigm.*

If philosophy is to be more than an academic exercise then it has to have pragmatic applications; without these, it would be effectively meaningless and pointless.

The pragmatic applications do not have to be immediately useful but could have the potential to be useful in the future. There is an analogy in the domains of theoretical physics and mathematics in which, when discoveries were first made, they had no particular pragmatic use, but were subsequently found to be extremely useful, for example, the structure of the atom in physics and complex numbers in mathematics.

So, in this chapter, I want to discuss some of the uses or at least some potential uses of a good philosophy. If a philosophical paradigm does not fulfil at least some of these uses, then it cannot be considered to be a good philosophy.

I am specifying a 'good' philosophy because a poor philosophy only skims over the surface and may have no uses at all. Also, any practical applications drawn from a poor or inaccurate philosophy may do more harm than good.

A good philosophy is one that is based upon explicit and irrefutable foundations and with clear processes of logical inference.

So what are the eleven uses of a good philosophy?

### 1.   Creating a better model of the world

We all have a model of the world that we use to make decisions and interact with the world. Having an understanding of the logic that underpins the process by which this model is created can be extremely useful in creating a better model of the world and hence also to make better decisions.

This is in the same way that understanding how a bicycle works is conducive to maintaining and riding the bicycle more effectively.

The pattern paradigm provides this understanding through its logical algorithm for pattern identification. It also highlights how the consideration of many possibilities is conducive to identifying the 'best' pattern to fit the relevant data.

### 2.   Creating a better model of abstract systems such as mathematics

It is extremely useful to distinguish and separate abstract systems such as pure mathematics from real systems which are based on sense-data. The two systems use very different logical processes of inference and conflating the two causes many logical problems.

For example, problems with Gödel's incompleteness theorems disappear as there is no requirement for completeness nor is there any requirement for 'truth'. (Theorems of the mathematical system can be labelled as being 'true within the system', but there is no requirement for it.)

### 3.  Understanding the foundations of science

Having a good understanding of the foundations of the scientific process, which are rooted in pattern identification, is essential for understanding the philosophy of science.

Problems of induction disappear as all of science is based upon pattern identification. There is no requirement for a perfect 'truth'.

The 'laws of physics' describe the motion and interactions of matter; matter does not 'obey' the 'laws of physics'.

Even the problems of Schroedinger's cat are resolved when one realises that it is only within one's incomplete model of the world, that there is a probability that the cat is either alive or dead.

### 4.  Understanding oneself and other people

A good philosophy will describe the world and its people and their thinking in simple and fundamental terms. This should provide a better understanding of people's actions and their motivations.

A fundamental tenet of the Pattern Paradigms is that everyone always seeks to maximise their own personal happiness. This can be useful for identifying and understanding people's motives and whether their claims and statements are honest.

(Note: I am using the term 'happiness' as a label for the experience of that to which the brain aspires. See Chapter 12: 'The Logic of Decision-Making' for more details.)

### 5.  Making better decisions

The prime function of the brain is as a decision-making device. Having an understanding of the logical process by which decisions are made can facilitate the effectiveness of the process.

The Pattern Paradigm describes an algorithm which models this process. One of the implications of the algorithm is that the more options considered and the deeper and more accurate the envisaged consequences, the better will be the decision eventually reached.

## 6. Refuting erroneous claims

Perhaps one of the most important benefits of having a good philosophy is to be able to evaluate the accuracy of beliefs and possibilities presented by other people. For this, the philosophy needs to have firm and indubitable foundations with clear processes of inference.

So if an idea presented by another does not fit with one's philosophical framework, then there are good grounds for rejecting it.

The world is full of misleading ideas, some of which are forcefully insisted upon, and if they don't make sense then they need to be refuted using firm foundations and clear logic, as presented by a good philosophy.

The Pattern Paradigm presents clear and irrefutable foundations and clear processes of logical inference that create a firm framework.

## 7. Creating a personalised philosophy

Everyone is different and unique. What works for one person in one place and time does not necessarily work for a different person in a different place and time. People's personalised philosophy needs to be tailored to fit their particular circumstances.

The Pattern Paradigm describes the bare bones of the logic of life. It allows others to flesh it out with what they have learnt from their own experiences. It does not claim, as do so many other philosophies, to be the truth, nor does it claim that others should simply believe what is being asserted. Instead, the Pattern Paradigm allows for flexibility in how it is fleshed out.

## 8. Achieving peace of mind

I suspect that for many people the attainment of a degree of peace of mind is one of their main motivations for delving into the domain of philosophy. In early adulthood one enters a world of complexity where there is a confusion of ideas that seem reasonable in isolation but which don't make sense when one tries to fit them together. The discontinuities of conflicting ideas can cause schisms in one's pyramids of patterns which can make rational thought difficult.

An example of a schism would be something like what many children are taught in society: 'one should always put other people first', which could conflict with one's own aim of personal happiness. The Pattern Paradigm aims to facilitate the construction of a personal model of the world from the deepest foundations to the conscious mind that is clear and without discontinuities. In this way, one may be able to make sense of the world and one's place within it and hence achieve peace of mind.

## 9.  Effecting therapies

As an analogy, it is not necessary to know the details of human anatomy for one's body to work effectively; however, it is very useful for a physician to know the details of human anatomy if they are to propose remedies should things go awry. So too is it for the logic of human thinking: It is not necessary for a person to understand the logic of human thinking in order to think effectively; however, it would be very useful for a psychotherapist to know the details of the logic of thinking in order to suggest remedies, should things go awry.

All too often in the modern world, things do go awry. People with perfect physical health can suffer anxiety and depression and perhaps subsequently tend towards self-harm, take mood-enhancing drugs of various kinds or even contemplate suicide. Clearly, these are problems of thinking rather than any physical problems within their brains, so it would be beneficial for a psychotherapist to understand the logic of thinking in order to suggest possible therapies.

So, for example, it may be that someone is suffering from a surfeit of schisms in their pyramid of patterns which is causing problems in thinking and decision-making. So it would be useful to diagnose this problem as the basis for finding a therapy.

## 10.  Creating a positive attitude towards life

It is all too easy to buy into poor but popular philosophies that promote despondency and a negative attitude towards life. But it doesn't have to be that way.

A good philosophy will endow a person with a positive attitude towards life; one in which one is master of one's own destiny and can always make decisions to improve one's lot in life and one's personal happiness.

A good philosophy, founded on deep and indubitable foundations, will give a person the confidence and skills to refute those who bemoan the futility of life.

We have all been given the wonderful gift of life; and the potential to appreciate that gift and lead a wonderful life. The Pattern Paradigm eschews despondency and instead promotes fun, imagination and laughter.

## 11. A platform for further exploration of philosophy

A good philosophy, such as The Pattern Paradigm, will describe the foundations and logical processes by which a model of the world can be created. Using this basic framework, someone who wishes to explore the ideas of philosophy further can expand the ideas into new domains or perhaps fill in some of the details. Some of these domains might include politics and sociology.

In the philosophical journey that I have been describing in this book, I have only gone over the bare bones of the framework of the ideas. There is plenty of opportunity for others to undertake their own journey of exploration and fill in some of the details. I have certainly found this journey of exploration of ideas to be fascinating, and I dare say that others could do the same.

# Chapter 23
# What Is the Logic of Imagination, and Why Is It So Important?

*We now take a look at and explore the role of imagination in life and in particular its role in the logic of fundamental perception.*

Imagination is an essential component of the process of making sense of the world. It is necessary at the very depths of perception when working out how to interpret raw data from the senses, especially the eyes. For it is found in the logic of the fundamental pattern identification algorithm described in Chapter 8 'Patterns, Time and Space' that is used for creating ideas out of sense-data.

The algorithm is one of pattern identification. It looks for patterns within the data. Intrinsic to that algorithm is a process of imagination.

Imagination is a necessary part of the algorithm as there is no deductive process for simply taking sense-data and extracting from it the best pattern to fit the data. There necessarily has to be a process of trial and error or more accurately a process of imagination and testing.

Here is the algorithm that describes the process, reproduced from Chapter 8

**Simple algorithm for pattern identification.**

1. Assemble the data
2. Input a template (e.g. a sample of the data
3. Test the template; does it fit?
4. If it doesn't fit return to step 2
5. Else continue
6. Store the template together with a label for the data.

I wish to draw attention to line 2: Input a template.

A template in this instance is a trial pattern, one that is to be tested according to whether it fits the data or not.

This pattern identification process is the only possible way of converting sense-data into concepts.

It is in the acquisition of trial templates that imagination is necessary.

But what is the logic of this imagination? How can a template be created?

In the very early stages of pattern identification when interpreting sense-data and beginning to create a model of the world there are only two possibilities for creating a possible template.

1. One can have an entirely random template.
2. One could use a sample of the data.
   Subsequently when a number of patterns have been identified, a third and fourth possibility arise:
3. One can use a pattern or template that fits an entirely different set of data; for example, one that fits one of the other senses.
4. Or perhaps a combination of one or more of the first three.

It is important to note that there is no limit to what can be used as a template for the pattern identification process. So, for example, one could use something

156

of the form: 'everything is made of water', 'the Moon is made of cheese' or 'time slows down the faster you travel through space'.

The reason there is no limit to the range of possible templates is that if the template is no good, it will not fit the data in the testing stage and can be subsequently discarded.

There is only a pragmatic limitation to considering various templates and that is in the amount of processing time required. For to assemble many possible templates and then test each of them against the data can be a very time-consuming process.

Testing a template against the data is a bit like a filter system whereby only the templates which have a reasonable fit to the data will get through and the rest are discarded. Note that the best patterns are ones that not only fit the data but also can reproduce the data.

Without this Imaginative source of templates and filter system for testing templates, there can be no pattern identification, and hence, no model of the world can be created.

This process of imagination and filtering is not too dissimilar from the trial-and-error process of genetic evolution. In genetic evolution, there is random variation of the genetic code within a particular genome which is subsequently tested in the associated phenotype as to whether it provides an advantage or a disadvantage with regard to the survivability of the organism; i.e. its ability to survive, thrive and procreate. If it is disadvantageous the organism will not survive, thrive and procreate and the genetic variation will disappear from the gene pool; whereas if it is advantageous then the genetic variation will remain within the gene pool.

Imagination is also important in the logic of decision-making. An algorithm describing this process was described in Chapter 12 'The Logic of Decision-Making'.

Here are the first few lines of the algorithm, reproduced from Chapter 12:

*Start of Decision-Making Algorithm*

1. *Assemble all possible actions for this decision.*
2. *Select one possible action.*
3. *Assemble all possible consequences of this action.*

The imaginative part of the algorithm resides in line 1 of the algorithm, which requires the collation of possible decisions together with their associated actions. Again there is no limit to the range of possible decisions that can be considered, for those whose likely outcome does not benefit the decision-maker will be discarded and only those likely to bring benefit need to be considered in depth.

A different form of imagination is required for the evaluation of the expected happiness for a particular decision and its associated action. It is one that requires an abstract visualisation of the consequences of a potential decision and its subsequent impact on one's personal happiness. It also requires a good model of the world in order to make accurate predictions of the potential consequences. So, for this to be effective, one needs to visualise or imagine the possible consequences.

Having chosen a decision and put it into action it is important to evaluate the actual consequences to see if they align with the predicted consequences and then to learn from that for making subsequent decisions. Though that said, caution must be exercised as we live in a complex world that it is full of change and quasi-random variations. So the same decision made another time in similar circumstances to a previous decision may produce entirely different consequences. So, for example, a child can run across a busy road without being hit by a car, but this is little indication that at another time they will achieve the same happy outcome.

There is another aspect of imagination, one where there is the creation of possibilities as before, but this time without the filtering system of fitting the possibilities to the facts of the real world. They are often manifest in what are termed the arts; i.e. music, abstract paintings, abstract sculptures, novels, poetry and so on. These remain only as possibilities and reside in a sort of fantasy world that has no direct correlation to the world of reality.

Even as fantasies, these can act as a communication from the artist to the viewer as a stimulus to the imagination and to open the viewer to the realm of possibilities.

Imagination is an intrinsic part of the human mind. From the roots of perception when infants seek to make sense of the mass of confusing sense-data that they are confronted with to the important decisions that people make in their lives to the trivial game of looking at clouds and suggesting animals or other shapes that they may bring to mind; the logic of imagination is paramount.

Imagination is important as it is inherent in the fundamental and underlying process that has brought about the huge technological advances that differentiate the modern world from that of the hunter-gatherer lifestyle of our ancient ancestors. Without our powers to exploit the logic of imagination, we would still be swinging through the trees.

Without imagination, one can do no more than follow the paths created by others, and while there is nothing wrong with that, some people want something more. Perhaps it is also important that people use their powers of imagination in order to fulfil their potential as human beings.

Finally, it may be of interest to note that other modern philosophies (i.e. philosophies other than The Pattern Paradigm) typically ignore imagination or even try to suppress it. They do not encourage imaginative ideas or innovation.

But so long as there are people who use their powers of imagination and promote new ideas and innovation, imagination can never be suppressed.

# Chapter 24
# Why Is Laughter So Important?

*We now turn to the uniquely human characteristic of laughter and its association with paradigm shifts.*

While there are many causes and aspects of laughter I only want to look at a few of them in this chapter.

Before looking at laughter specifically, I would first like to look at its underlying logical causes and in order to do this we shall have to dive into the depths of fundamental cognition.

It was mooted in Chapter 8: 'Patterns, Time and Space' that the only way for a logical processor to begin to make sense of the world is through the logical process of pattern identification.

The essence of the logic of the pattern identification process resides in posing or imagining possible patterns and then testing them against the data to determine which one of them is the best fit to the data.

The 'best' pattern is the one that is simplest and most accurate; or in other words, it is the best compression of the data without losing too much accuracy. Inherent in the process is the fact that one can only ever find the best pattern, one can never be sure that there is not a better pattern somewhere that might be found which fits the data more simply and more accurately. So what this means is that once the best pattern has been found, it may be the case that later, perhaps much later, when more data has been found or a better possible pattern identified, one arrives at a better pattern than one's original best pattern. The patterns one uses to create a model of the world are not permanent; they may need adjusting at a later time. When this occurs, it can be labelled as a 'pattern-shift'.

Typically these pattern-shifts can occur in one of two ways. Either more data is received which does not fit the original pattern, or secondly, it may be that a better possible pattern is suggested which fits the data better than the original pattern.

In this way, an old pattern may be replaced by a new and better one. And sometimes these pattern-shifts can produce the physical response of laughter.

As an example of the first type of pattern-shift where the shift comes about through new data being received, perhaps you see a friend in a crowded room that you have not seen for a while; so you go over to them and give them a warm greeting... only to realise... 'oops'... they are not the person you thought they were... so you both laugh at the mistaken identity and to ease any awkward social tension.

An example of the second type of pattern-shift, where a better possible pattern is suggested, can be found in the children's riddle of: 'Why do birds fly south?' Given this scenario, one might consider various reasons why birds fly south, such as that they seek warmer weather or a better supply of food. But none of these answers seem to be convincing. So when the answer is given: 'Because it is too far to walk!' one realises that this concise answer fits perfectly, albeit in an unusual way. The answer constitutes the best pattern to fit the data. It is a possible pattern which when tested against the data of the scenario is found to fit perfectly. And when compared to the possible answers that one had been searching for, the sudden realisation of the identification of the best pattern can induce the physical response of laughter.

One can then ask the question: Why does this physical response of laughter occur and why is it pleasurable?

There are a number of possible reasons for this:

Firstly, the enjoyment of laughing may be because one is exercising the mind, and this is pleasurable and beneficial to one's mind in a similar way that exercising one's limbs, especially in the form of physical activity, is enjoyable and beneficial to one's physical body.

Secondly, the physical response may also be for the purpose of communication; the communication that one has got the joke or understands the witty remark. It may also be a matter of sharing and showing that one has a similar understanding with other people who also laugh.

Thirdly, the process may be enjoyable because one realises that one has just made better sense of the world.

While jokes and laughter are usually associated with words, it is not the words themselves that generate the laughter; instead, it is the patterns that the words are linked to and a shift in those patterns that creates the laughter.

While jokes, witticisms and misunderstandings are trivial and can provide minor amusement, there can also be pattern-shifts or shifts in ideas that can be life-changing.

It was discussed in Chapter 9: 'Pyramids, Patterns and Why We Sleep', how one constructs a model of the world by creating patterns of patterns.

These patterns of patterns are built from the ground up and form a pyramid of patterns where each pattern is linked to other patterns, with the fundamental patterns of perception at the base level and higher patterns of cognition and interrelated ideas at higher levels. Ideally, this pyramid of patterns will have a high degree of self-consistency.

If a pattern-shift occurs that is deep in the pyramid of patterns it can have a ripple effect on all the patterns above it. This can occur when some new data comes along which is at variance with the original data that was available when the pattern was formed, or it can occur when a new possible pattern or template is imagined by oneself or suggested by another and which fits the available data more accurately and more simply than the original pattern.

When one constructs a model of the world using pattern identification, that is not the end of it. As one acquires more data and ideas, these need to be fitted in smoothly with what one already knows. However, sometimes this is not possible and a shift of ideas is required in order to maintain the harmony of one's pyramid of patterns.

An example of some new data that does not fit easily into one's pyramid of patterns could be that one realises that a trusted close friend has told a significant lie and so much of what that person has said in the past has to be re-evaluated as being possibly a lie as well. So the simple pattern-shift could have a ripple effect on one's other beliefs as well. This could even result in the total re-evaluation of one's beliefs about that person as being a trustworthy friend. So the original pattern-shift could turn into a more complicated paradigm shift; in other words a major shift to all one's beliefs about that person.

A paradigm is a collection of self-consistent ideas or patterns; so then a paradigm shift is a shift in many or all of these ideas. For example, science is a paradigm, philosophy is a paradigm and to some degree one's pyramid of patterns constitutes a paradigm. For they all constitute a collection of ideas or patterns which are interconnected and ultimately and ideally are required to be self-consistent. Then if one of the ideas within the paradigm gets re-evaluated and shifted, this can have repercussions for the whole of the paradigm as the patterns are shifted around in order to maintain self-consistency within the paradigm; this is called a paradigm shift. The deeper in the pyramid of patterns that a pattern-shift occurs, the greater the paradigm shift.

As another example, there is the famous children's story about the ugly duckling, in which a duckling is teased by the other ducklings as being ugly. This continues until one day he realises that he is actually a beautiful swan and not an ugly duckling at all. This paradigm shift did not come about through additional data but by the realisation of the possibility of him being a swan and that this idea was a better fit to the data than his original belief that he was a duckling. This was confirmed when he looked at his reflection in the water. Such paradigm shifts can also occur with human children as they grow up and realise that they are neither ugly nor defective in some way but actually beautiful human beings. This can greatly enhance one's self-image as a person.

Then there are the more well-known paradigm shifts such as when it was mooted in the seventeenth century in Europe that the theory that the Earth goes around the Sun constituted a simpler and more accurate pattern than the previously existing popular belief that the Sun orbits the Earth. The proposed paradigm shift caused great consternation at that time, particularly among the Catholic church. The church did not want to re-evaluate its perceived position of man and the Earth being at the centre of the universe and so tried to reject and suppress the new idea. But ultimately, of course, the new theory prevailed, as it was a better pattern to fit the data. Nowadays, the idea that the Sun orbits the Earth seems ridiculous and if someone seriously suggested that the Sun orbits the Earth, we would simply laugh as the theory does not begin to fit the data.

A shift in a person's deep patterns can be disturbing, as this may require a considerable amount of re-evaluating of the patterns in one's personal pyramid of patterns; especially if the pattern-shift occurs to a pattern that was originally held to be 'true'. While such a paradigm shift may be disturbing, it is also productive and beneficial as it leads to one having a better model of the world and hence enhances one's ability to make better decisions and achieve better happiness.

It may also occur that this re-evaluation of patterns, following a deep paradigm shift, may produce laughter as one realises that things that did not make sense before are now starting to make sense, and there is pleasure associated with this.

These paradigm shifts and associated laughter can only take place within a person's pyramid of patterns, where one idea is linked to another in a holistic pyramid of understanding. In contrast, where there is only rote learning of configurations of words as in a recipe or formula or popular cliché, there is no understanding, and hence, there can be no laughter.

For if one has a well-constructed and well-functioning pyramid of patterns that is free of discontinuities or schisms, then one can play around with ideas and have fun with them, and see what makes sense and what does not, and perhaps even invoke laughter.

To some extent, this is what 'The Pattern Paradigm' philosophy that I have been describing in this book is all about. I am presenting possible patterns that people might find fit the available data more simply and more accurately than their previous patterns or rote learning; hence enabling them to make better sense of the world and to create for themselves a better model of the world. I am not claiming, of course, that these patterns are the best possible; I am only claiming that they are the best patterns that are currently available. (When I came to the realisation that the new patterns fitted the data so much better than the old, I found myself laughing. Perhaps others will do so too.)

As a final note, there has been a lot of talk about artificial intelligence, AI, recently and fears about how it might take over the world. However, there is

nothing to fear from AI, at least not until such time as they develop a sense of humour; something that they are currently far from achieving. A sense of humour is an indication of a well-structured and well-functioning pyramid of patterns and a pyramid of patterns is an essential requirement for an effective model of the world. Without an effective model of the world, AI is nothing more than a mindless machine. While such a machine can be destructive, in the way that a runaway train can be destructive, it could not begin to take over the world. So until such time as there is evidence that AI has developed an effective model of the world and is capable of laughter, there is nothing to worry about.

Pattern-shifts and paradigm shifts and their associated laughter are essential ingredients for maintaining a healthy pyramid of patterns and an accurate model of the world. Laughter is an indication that one has a well-functioning pyramid of patterns.

# Chapter 25

# Why an Apple? Knowing vs Understanding

*We now turn to exploring the all-important distinction between knowing and understanding.*

I will start with a couple of quotes. The first is attributed, albeit questionably, to Albert Einstein: 'Any fool can know, the point is to understand.'

And this from the physicist Richard Feynman: 'I don't know what is the matter with people, they don't learn by understanding they learn some other way – by rote or something; their knowledge is so fragile.'

In brief 'knowing' typically resides in the domain of words in the form of an arrangement of words such as 'apples grow on trees'.

Whereas understanding resides in the domain of inter-connecting patterns such as the relationship between trees, fruits and seeds, and fitting these concepts into a cohesive whole.

One needs an understanding of the world in order to create a good model of the world. And one needs a good model of the world in order to make good decisions. And one needs to make good decisions in order to achieve happiness. So understanding is important.

Understanding, within the logic of the mind, requires a pyramid of patterns. A pyramid of patterns is a hierarchy of ideas in the mind that constitutes a person's model of the world. Understanding requires that these ideas and concepts are linked together in a cohesive and harmonious way. One's pyramid of patterns is founded on sense-data and the logical process of pattern identification. (This process was described in Chapter 8 'Patterns, Time and Space' and also in Chapter 9: 'Pyramids, Patterns and Why We Sleep'.)

The relationship between words and patterns is that words are labels for patterns. This was discussed in Chapter 16 'Words, Language and Communication'. If one only knows the words without understanding the patterns beneath those words and how they fit together with other patterns in one's pyramid of patterns, then one doesn't understand the concepts that the words purport to represent; all one knows is an arrangement of labels.

There may be a number of reasons for a person not having an understanding of the words. It could be that they do not have sufficient knowledge about the domain to which the words refer in order to make sense of the words. Or perhaps the words do not refer to a meaningful domain of the real world at all and are fictional. Or perhaps the words are simply inherently meaningless. (Incidentally, when I refer to the 'real world', I mean the one that can ultimately be linked to sense-data.)

An example of knowing the words but without understanding them is artificial intelligence and the recent ChatGPT program. Artificial intelligence may know many of the words and how the words are linked to other words, but it has no concept of the patterns beneath the words for it has no pyramid of patterns. Neither is it linked in any way to sense-data and the real world. And because of this it has no understanding and cannot delve beyond its programmed instructions. Even if Artificial intelligence does have rudimentary links to sense-data from the real world in the way that self-drive vehicles do, It can still only follow its programmed instructions in an entirely mindless way that is devoid of understanding.

So what is there to understand? What can be understood? There are two main divisions of understandable knowledge. One is what I call 'abstract systems', which includes purely logical systems such as mathematics and the game of chess. This was described in Chapter 13: 'Abstract Systems'.

The other branch of understandable knowledge is 'real systems', which is a logical system of pattern identification based on sense-data and which is incorporated into one's pyramid of patterns. Both of these systems have firm foundations and explicit processes of inference by which one idea can be linked to another. (Incidentally, the relationship between the two systems is one of a mapping whereby the elements of an abstract system can be mapped onto elements of the real system, and vice versa.)

This division into two systems is echoed by David Hume (and also others) when he wrote: 'All the objects of human reason may be divided into two kinds: relations of ideas and matters of fact'. So what Hume referred to as 'relations of ideas', I am calling 'abstract systems' and his 'matters of fact' as a 'real system'.

Both of these systems can be explored and are open to understanding.

As previously mentioned, understanding and having a good model of the world is important as it facilitates good decision-making and one needs to make good decisions in order to achieve happiness.

The difference between knowing and understanding in the domain of abstract systems can be demonstrated by this example in mathematics: one might know perhaps that in calculus the gradient of the graph of $y=x^2$ is given by $2x$. And these words and symbols may be known and the gradient of $2x$ can be used. However, in order to achieve an understanding of the calculus and of how it fits in with the rest of the mathematical system, one would need to be able to derive the theorem that the gradient of $y=x^2$ is given by $2x$ from the basic axioms and rules of mathematics.

In the domain of real systems, one may know, for example, how a car works in terms of pressing the accelerator to make the car go forward and pressing the brake pedal to make the car slow down. But this is simple surface knowledge. To actually understand how a car works requires deeper knowledge, and there are many levels of deeper knowledge. So, for example, at the next level down one might understand how the combustion of fuel and air in a confined space can create kinetic energy which can be used to rotate the prop shaft which in turn can be used to rotate the wheels and push the car forward. At a still deeper level, one can have an understanding of how the pistons operate within the cylinders with their valves, camshafts and ignition sources. And this understanding could prove to be useful should there be a problem or breakdown of the car.

Understanding lies in looking at the nuts and bolts of a phenomenon and how those nuts and bolts fit together. Most anything that belongs to the real world is understandable.

But what about things that fall outside of these two categories of logical abstract systems and real systems?

Well, such things would lie in the world of fiction or fantasy or perhaps historical tradition. If they reside only in the world of words, then they cannot be broken down into nuts and bolts and become understandable, there is only a simple knowledge of the words themselves.

Some people do live in a world of words without even attempting to understand the nuts and bolts. Certainly, such people can lead happy and fulfilling lives, but they may be living in an artificial world in which people simply follow the rituals and traditions of their culture without understanding what their purpose or usefulness is.

As Feynman alluded, it is a fragile world because without deep foundations, it is subject to the whims of fashion, public opinion and perhaps the assertions of charlatans.

This relates to the schisms that were discussed in Chapter 17 'Culture and Schisms', where it was discussed how some words and ideas that are embedded in historical culture may not seem to fit within one's pyramid of patterns, and so they cannot be understood. Their only reality is that they are a part of popular historical culture. They lack the foundations based on the real world and sense-data.

David Hume considered that such writings about fantasy worlds that didn't fit in with either of his two categories should be committed to the flames as in his famous quote: 'If we take in hand any volume, let us ask: Does it contain any abstract reasoning containing quantity or number? No. Does it contain any experimental reasoning concerning matters of fact and existence? No. Commit it then to the flames, for it can contain nothing but sophistry and illusion'.

While I wouldn't say that such volumes should be cast into the flames, they can certainly be regarded as fiction, fantasy or illusion. But so long as it is realised that they belong to the world of fiction or fantasy and not the real world, then they do have a place in the human world. Such fiction can be a stimulus to the imagination and open up a world of possibility and hence, in this way, provide a useful function.

Much of Standard Western Philosophy resides in the domain of words, which makes it highly resistant to understanding.

So what can one do to explore a particular real phenomenon or situation and turn mere knowledge into understanding? Well, first, one has to identify what the real phenomenon is, as distinct from the mere words. For words themselves cannot be analysed as they are merely labels. The question 'Why?' Is a good one to use as it is a request for more information and a motivation to delve beneath the surface. Also, the question 'How?' is a good one as in 'How do things fit together?' as it motivates one to look at the links between the nuts and bolts of the system.

As an example, I would like to ask the question 'Why an apple?' as portrayed in the picture at the start of this chapter. (Incidentally I am here paraphrasing Chico Marx's famous line 'Why a duck?'.) One can know that an apple is good to eat and can be found on an apple tree or perhaps find it for sale in a shop. But to understand what an apple actually is, one has to examine the reality of the apple and not just the words that describe its surface appearance and some of its uses. One has to analyse the entity itself and break it up into its component parts as I have shown schematically in the picture. In this way, one can discover for oneself its structure and its constituent parts.

So the first task is to divide the apple into its constituent parts, examine each in turn and hence gain an understanding of how the parts fit together.

At the heart of the apple are its pips or seeds. And once one has found the seed and has an understanding of the constituent parts of the apple, one can reverse the process of analysis and construct a synthesis. So instead of dividing the apple into its constituent parts one can start at the centre, which in this case is the basic seed and then construct an understandable story for how, starting from the foundation of the seed, one can construct an explanation for why an apple exists.

The story one might arrive at, put very simply, could be that the seed contains the genetic material required for the apple tree to reproduce. And plants and trees require some mechanism by which they can spread their seeds far and wide so that the new seedlings don't have to try to grow where they fall, underneath the shade of their parent tree. Apple trees have come up with the solution of putting their seeds in fruits which are attractive to local animals so that when those animals eat the fruit they will carry the seeds far from the tree and the seeds will eventually pass through the animal and be excreted onto the ground together with some manure to nourish the young apple trees. In understanding this, the ideas are linked to other ideas about the world such as evolution, animals, growth and the incredible diversity of life.

I should note here that understanding about the world is not certainty about the world; instead, it is about making sense of the world. Understanding opens up the possibility of new and greater understanding; whereas simple certainty is a barrier to learning.

In the Pattern Paradigm philosophy that I have been describing in this book, I have tried to focus on understanding rather than simple knowing. I have constructed a synthesis that starts from a few fundamental ideas and shown, using only the simplest of words, how these ideas can be linked together and expanded into a philosophy of logical thinking and of how people create a model of the world and how people interact with the world.

In the process of analysing the domain of philosophy and before constructing the synthesis, I examined the tenets and ideas of other popular Western philosophies but found that many of them did not fit within either of the two systems of knowledge of the abstract system or the real system and hence rejected them as belonging only to a fantasy world and hence ignored them when constructing the synthesis described in this book.

So to summarise, knowing is contained in an arrangement of words, whereas understanding is to be found by exploring the relationship between the nuts and bolts that constitute this world. Understanding leads to the creation of a better and more useful model of the world.

# Chapter 26
# The Human Dichotomy: Fantasy vs Reality

*We now come to the part of our journey where we explore the fascinating domain of fantasy vs reality and how they may be distinguished.*

In this chapter, I want to discuss something of a tricky topic, yet it is an important one. It relates to the model of the world which we create for ourselves, and which is inherent to all of us. Within that model, there are elements of reality and elements of fantasy. It is important to be able to distinguish reality from fantasy in order to make better sense of the world and especially for interacting effectively with the world.

So diving right in, we can start with exploring the question of what is reality and where does it come from. The only link that our brains have to the world of reality is through our senses. Without our senses, we would be locked into an abstract and meaningless world of chaos. So it is only through our senses that we can begin to make sense of the world of reality.

The only logical process by which our brains can begin to make sense of the data from our senses is through the logical process of pattern identification. This process was first introduced in Chapter 8: 'Patterns, Time and Space'. It was continued in Chapter 9: 'Pyramids, Patterns and Why We Sleep', where it was shown how a recursive application of the logical process of pattern identification can be used to create a hierarchy of patterns; one which I call a pyramid of patterns. This pyramid of patterns is effectively equivalent to one's model of the world.

The essence of the pattern identification process is to identify a pattern that fits the data without losing too much accuracy and in this way extract information about the nature of reality. In mathematical terms this is a compression of the data; the amount of information required to describe the pattern needs to be less than that required to describe the raw data (otherwise, it does not constitute a compression and no pattern has been found). If the identified pattern is a good fit for the data, then it can also be used to recreate the data.

This model of the world that we create from patterns is, in effect, the world in which we live; it constitutes all that we know about reality; the world beyond our senses.

The efficacy of our model of the world is affirmed by our ability to use the model to interact with the world in order to meet our physical needs of warmth, food and so on. In this way, our model of the world that is encapsulated in our pyramid of patterns, is considered to be real. This was discussed in Chapter 10: 'The Foundations of Reality and Purpose'.

However, sometimes the patterns that are considered to be the best available may in fact be very crude and are not able to fit the data accurately and efficiently; nor are they able to reproduce the data. Also, sometimes the form of the pattern itself is so complex that it does not compress the data. Such poor patterns are best considered as mere possibilities or if they are very poor, as fantasies. A fantasy is an idea that has very little connection to reality. Nevertheless, these poor outcomes are common when trying to identify patterns from the data.

In considering the distinction between fantasy and reality it would seem that there is no clear dividing line between the two. It is perhaps best considered as a continuum with absolute fantasies at one end and absolute reality at the other, and with possibilities somewhere in the middle.

| | | |
|---|---|---|
| I | I | I |
| Absolute<br>fantasy | Possibilities | Absolute<br>reality |

I would now like to turn to the decision-making process that is used by people to interact with the real world. This was discussed in Chapter 12: 'The Logic of Decision-Making'. The aim of the brain in this decision-making process is to maximise its happiness, in both the short term and long term. This aim of happiness is not so much a goal as it is a direction used to guide decision-making. The brain's aim of happiness is associated with the well-being of its physical body in terms of, for example, food, warmth and reproduction. The specific form of this happiness within a species or an individual will have been determined through the process of evolution.

All decisions are based upon this aim of happiness and apply not only to decisions regarding the movement of one's limbs but also to decisions of what to say and even to decisions regarding what to believe. A person will choose to believe whatever they consider will maximise their long-term happiness and perhaps also their short-term happiness. It is this choice of what to believe that is significant for this discussion.

Typically in our modern society, there are many ideas floating around that have but little connection to the real world. Often there are cultural and social pressures for a person to adopt these ideas as their own beliefs, even if they don't make a lot of sense.

Therein lies the human dichotomy: whether to believe only those things that one has learnt for oneself from one's own senses or to believe those things that don't really make sense but which other people seem to believe. Invariably people will choose those beliefs that they consider will maximise their happiness. Sometimes people will choose to believe ideas that are little more than fantasies.

To believe in fantasies is not necessarily a bad thing, for they can provide entertainment and personal comfort, a sense of community and perhaps guidelines for other decision-making. However, it is important not to hold them as firm or immutable beliefs, for they are, at best, just possibilities. Fantasies need to be recognised as fantasies and not claimed as truths nor extrapolated into the world of reality.

Typically such believed fantasies lie in the domains of religion, politics and people's own egos. For example, in religion, the concept of 'God' is highly complex and undefined; as such the theory of God does not compress the data. Neither can the concept of 'God' recreate the data. Hence the concept of God belongs more to the domain of fantasy or perhaps remote possibility than to the domain of reality. Nevertheless, for many people 'God' is fundamental to their beliefs and for them, God is 'real'

In politics, people often start from their own personal experience and seek generalised improvements, but surround their intentions with wordy justifications based upon cherry-picked data that belong more to the domain of fantasy than to the domain of reality. In politics, there is much propaganda and encouragement for people to believe the propaganda. Yet typically, the propaganda is just fantasy, as it is not based upon verifiable facts.

With regard to people's personal egos, many people like to believe that they are the best or that their culture, community or sports team is the best. However, not every person, culture or sports team can be the best. It is just wishful thinking to consider that they are the best. Hence such notions belong more in the domain of fantasy than in the domain of reality.

People choose to believe these fantasies for reasons that could include peer pressure or that it makes them feel good about themselves, or that they must be good things to believe as everyone else believes them. They choose the beliefs that they consider will maximise their personal happiness.

However, there are caveats to be considered with regard to believing fantasies.

First, there is no means of achieving consensus between people who disagree about their fantasies, as there cannot be any recourse to evaluating them in terms of the facts of the real world as they only exist in a fantasy world. So while specific communities of people can agree on their fantasies, a different community will inevitably have different fantasies, and there can be no rational path to agreement. Then if people are fanatical about their fantasy beliefs and consider them to be an integral part of who they are, as people, they may feel motivated to use violence to resolve their disagreement. This is evident in the many religious and political wars that have been fought over the centuries and still continue to this day. Also, as so often happens, a clash of personal egos can lead to violence.

The other problem with believing fantasies is that we actually live in the real world, and beliefs in fantasies are likely to lead to poor decisions and hence bring about a harder road to happiness.

Another problem with believing fantasies is that people will inevitably communicate and share their fantasies with other people, especially their children, in aspects of, for example, religion, politics and culture. Yet it is hard for a child to incorporate fantasies into their model of the world as fantasies cannot be easily integrated with the patterns that they have constructed from sense-data and which describe the real world.

This can lead to anomalies in their model of the world. These anomalies can create unsettling discontinuities in their pyramid of patterns, which can lead to psychological problems. This was discussed in Chapter 17 'Culture and Schisms'. Or alternatively, the child will simply believe these fantasies and have a distorted model of the world.

While there is a place for fantasies and for believing them in popular culture, there is no place for fantasies in philosophy; at least nothing more than the identification of them as fantasies. This is because, if for no other reason, philosophy has no goal of happiness.

In philosophy, if something is identified as being unknown with no good pattern to fit the data; rather than indulging in fanciful thinking and allowing a fantasy to fill the gap, that unknown something is best simply tagged as being 'unknown' which would then allow for further investigation and exploration.

Nevertheless, Standard Western philosophy, which primarily exists in the world of words, does not delve beneath the level of words to the world of reality and sense-data. Neither do its theories have the capability of reproducing the data. As such, it cannot be claimed that its theories belong to the domain of reality; instead, they can be considered as belonging to the domain of fantasy.

In contrast, the Pattern Paradigm philosophy that I have been describing in this book fits well with the facts of the world and sense-data. I have also put it in such an explicit and simple form that anyone can follow the paths of inference to reach the same conclusions. Hence the Pattern Paradigm can be considered to lie in the domain of reality.

So how can one identify a fantasy and distinguish it from the domain of reality?

The domain of reality is founded on pattern identification of sense-data. Any ideas or patterns that can be linked directly or through a series of logical inferences to pattern identification of sense-data can be considered to be a part of the real world. Any ideas or theories that do not meet this requirement can be considered to lie in the domain of fantasy.

Perhaps an example would be useful to illustrate this: consider electrons and ghosts.; are they fantasies or real?

The evidence that electrons are part of the world of reality is explicit and public. The data and the logical inferences used to infer their existence can be reproduced by anyone with sufficient interest and motivation to do so. It would incorporate ideas and experiments about electric charge and the quantisation of charge. Other experiments could determine mass. If such experiments were re-enacted it is most likely that the conclusion reached would be that there is a particle within the domain of reality that can be identified and labelled as an 'electron'. Electrons are a pattern that can be linked directly to sense-data.

Ghosts are a different matter, however. The evidence for ghosts is exclusively hearsay; people have stories about encountering strange phenomena and then they imaginatively interpret them as being created by 'ghosts'. However, people's stories about such things cannot be relied upon. There are no experiments that indicate the existence of ghosts nor places one could go where one is likely to encounter a ghost. Nothing about ghosts can definitively be linked to facts or sense-data. As such the theory of ghosts can unequivocally be consigned to the domain of fantasy.

The dichotomy between fantasy and reality is a uniquely human predicament. Humans uniquely have a comprehensive language, and without a comprehensive language, there would be no world of fantasy; there would only be a world of reality.

I daresay that some people prefer living in a mostly fantasy world, but in that case, they are reliant on other people who live in a mostly real world to fulfil their material needs.

Ultimately, we live in a world of reality, and so it is important to identify and separate the world of reality from the world of fantasy and to make decisions based on the world of reality.

# Chapter 27
# Where Is Freedom?

*We are now getting towards the end of our journey, and we are now ready to explore the domain of freedom; how freedom can be attained and why it is important.*

So what is freedom? Well, it can have a variety of meanings but the one that I will be using is that freedom is a state of mind: the ability to make choices and to make those choices free from fetters and restrictions. One can consider the state of mind of freedom to be akin to that of a seagull flying free on the breeze and making decisions without psychological fetters or restrictions.

The opposite of freedom, I shall call 'slavery'. I don't mean this in a physical sense where a person is an actual fettered slave but rather as a state of mind where one is a slave to perceived restrictions that seem to curtail one's freedom of choice.

To give an example of what I mean: Suppose someone has a job as an employee at some company where they are working for a boss. There are two ways they can view this. First, they are a slave to their job. They have no choice but to follow the instructions of their boss in order to keep their job and provide an income upon which they can survive.

Or alternatively, they can view the situation as one in which they have choices. They can consider themselves to be in a state of self-employment where their boss is their customer to whom they provide services and try to keep happy so that the company keeps paying them money. Then, if the situation is not to their satisfaction they have a choice to seek out a different customer to whom they can provide services and get paid. In the first state of mind, they are a slave without choices; in the second, they are free to make choices.

Another example is in the domain of addictions, whether benign or harmful. The addictions I am talking about could be anything from television to heroin from gambling to alcohol. The difference between freedom and slavery is whether a person has the addiction or the addiction has them. Suppose that the addiction has them, then they are a slave to their addiction; they have no choice but to submit to their addiction.

However, if instead they have the addiction, then they are free to choose to indulge in their addiction or to choose to let it go and do something else instead. Their choice will depend upon whether they consider the benefits of the addiction outweigh the downsides or not.

Freedom is the ability to make choices based upon what one knows about the world and what one considers will be most likely to bring one happiness in both the short term and the long term. It is all about the ability to make choices.

In Chapter 12, I described the logic of decision-making. Very briefly this was: for a situation which requires a decision, one considers all the possible actions that one might take and for each possible action, one evaluates all the possible consequences and their impact on one's happiness. Then one simply selects the decision most likely to bring one the greatest happiness. But this process is essentially for a free person. All too often in modern society, there are restrictions upon one's freedom of choice. I discussed this in Chapter 17 'Culture and Schisms' where I describe how culture can impose restrictions upon one's freedom of thinking and freedom of choice.

These schisms would include things like 'you should do this...', 'you shouldn't do that'. I refer to them as 'schisms' as they can act as a discontinuity in one's thinking and decision-making.

We live in a world of human activity where social customs and constraints seem to dominate people's thinking. It is far removed from the more natural world of our distant hunter-gatherer ancestors where social customs and constraints were effectively non-existent.

Some people might say that fitting in with social customs and mores is what life is all about, as society is paramount and the individual is of less importance. But this would be a naive viewpoint. Thinking and choices are processes that take place only within the minds of individuals.

When one is growing up, one has little choice but to adopt the culture of one's society and the values of one's parents or caregivers. For at that time, one has a very limited knowledge of the world and one lacks the means by which such culture and values can be evaluated as to their merits or lack thereof. So they simply exist as words in one's head, and as imperatives in one's decision-making; in other words, they are a barrier to one's freedom of choice.

It is only as one progresses in life and can understand the usefulness and limitations of society's mores, that they will cease to act as barriers to one's decision-making, but instead can be used as useful caveats or suggestions. Once this has been achieved, one can be free of their imposing influence. However, if this cannot be achieved, then one remains a slave to one's culture.

Freedom requires a good model of the world and an understanding of how the different elements, aspirations and restrictions all fit together. The process of understanding was discussed in Chapter 25 'Knowing vs Understanding'. Without a good model of the world and an understanding of how it functions, one is, in effect, making decisions in the dark.

Cultures and values are flexible and are not set in stone; they were created by ordinary people like you and me. The people who created them were following their own personal pursuit of happiness, and they may or may not have had the best intentions for other people. Since they are not set in stone, they can be modified to fit one's own experience and knowledge of the world, or alternatively one can simply accept them as they are. It is a matter of finding a balance between society and oneself.

Thinking takes place within an individual mind as does decision-making, so any ethical philosophy needs to place the individual at the heart of its ethics. It is pure folly to try to create a rigorous ethical system based upon society and group dynamics alone while ignoring the individual. This was discussed in Chapter 19 'Is Morality a Good Ethical System?'

However, the world is filled with ethical systems that put groups and societies at the heart of their ethics. This results in the world being permeated with what can be described as hand-waving propaganda. And by 'hand-waving' I mean using faulty logic or relying on subjective opinions. And propaganda is an attempt to get people to believe things for which there is scant evidence.

In this way, groups of people try to impose their vague values upon other people. But since they are without a firm foundation and rigorous logic, this can only be considered as propaganda, even if they try to bolster their questionable arguments by claiming that they are 'true'. In this way, they try to make slaves of us all. But there are no moral truths, there are only moral guidelines.

That said, there may still be some merit in the mores, propaganda and social etiquette as they can have pragmatic usefulness for the structure of a harmonious society. It is just that such mores, propaganda and etiquette are not set in stone; nor are they derivable from first principles. They are no more than empirical guidelines. (Incidentally, this is commensurate with David Hume's famous claim that you 'can't get a "should" from an "is".')

All mores need to be tailored for each particular society on the basis of what works best for the harmonious functioning of that society. It needs to be based on pragmatism rather than esoteric theory.

Should one choose to move away from mainstream mores and morality, one would need to proceed with caution. For there is much wisdom in the mores and etiquette of society, and there may well be risks involved in taking them at less than face value. Especially, one would need to take into account the laws of one's country, as these may have considerable influence on the consequences of one's actions and their possible effects upon one's own long-term happiness or indeed on one's short-term happiness.

Some people may well understand the situation and yet choose to remain within the mores of their society and that is their choice. It is certainly a safer option; while others may choose to push the boundaries and find out what might be possible.

The point I want to make is that it is a choice, a choice that can be freely made. Inevitably, a person will choose a course of action that they consider will bring them the most happiness.

One has the freedom to interpret what other people say in any way that one chooses. For example, one can choose to interpret what others say as being truth, hypocrisy, nonsense, lies, propaganda, fantasy or possibility. Of course, it would be simplest to interpret what others say as being essentially truthful, but this is not necessarily the most expedient choice.

It is also possible that some people may consider the tradition and scholarship of mainstream philosophy, which I call 'Standard Western Philosophy', to be beyond doubt as it appears to be so logical and established. However, I have shown in Chapter 18 'Disembodied Statements are Meaningless' and in Chapter 20 'What Is Truth?' how the assumptions of Standard Western Philosophy are unjustifiable and its logic is fatally flawed.

Incidentally, Standard Western Philosophy has no philosophy of freedom and, de facto, it would appear that any sort of freedom is anathema to them.

In effect, Standard Western Philosophy only exists in a sort of fantasy world where words without understanding predominate. By 'fantasy world' I mean a world that has no more relevance to the real world than 'Narnia' or 'Middle Earth'. While this may seem controversial, it is the only rational conclusion to draw regarding a philosophy that has such a tenuous connection to the real world as Standard Western Philosophy. Hence its tenets are, at the least, suspect and many of them are simply irrelevant. Should someone blindly and meekly accept the tenets of Standard Western Philosophy without understanding them then they can be considered to be a slave.

In place of this, I have developed The Pattern Paradigm philosophy which I have been describing in this book and which I claim is well founded in its assumptions, and which has a clear, explicit and simple logic. So this philosophy the 'Pattern Paradigm' can be used as a foundation for achieving freedom and for rejecting the propaganda of those who would try to restrict one's freedom.

At the heart of the Pattern Paradigm is the thinking of the individual. It follows from this that everyone has the freedom to make choices for themselves to achieve their personal happiness.

In conclusion: Everyone has an innate right to freedom. Freedom is the ability to pursue one's own happiness without hindrance or encumbrance from other people. And perhaps most importantly, freedom is the ability to use one's mind to its full capability. It is important to realise that one can be free; free to pursue one's own personal happiness and free to enjoy the magic of life.

Freedom is the natural state of mankind; and without that freedom, mankind risks losing its humanity.

# Chapter 28
# The Magic of Life

The Magic of Life

*In our journey, we now turn to explore ideas that cannot be explained in simpler terms. These are best described as magical.*

People typically like a bit of mystery and magic in their lives and complain that if they know how something works that the mystery and magic disappear. But this isn't really the case because what they have learnt takes them to a deeper level of understanding; nevertheless there are still deeper levels beyond that which can be explored. Or are there? Perhaps one eventually reaches places where no further understanding is possible.

As one learns about how things work in the world, one is not so much learning about the actual real world so much as one is learning about a model of the world, whether that is a model of physics or a model of biology or a philosophical model. There will always be things that are beyond that model, for eventually, one will arrive at places where no further progress or understanding is possible.

So, for example, the Pattern Paradigm that I have been describing in this book constitutes a model for the logic of thinking. It is a means of understanding the world, making sense of it and a model for interacting with the world. But it is not the world itself, it is only a model. The world itself is far more mysterious and wonderful than could ever be described in the words of a philosophy. It is something to be experienced and a good philosophy such as the Pattern Paradigm can enhance the experience.

In Chapter 25: 'Why an Apple?', the importance of understanding the nuts and bolts of how a thing works was emphasised. It was also claimed that if something is not understandable, in that it cannot be broken down into the nuts and bolts of its constituent parts, then that something belongs to a fantasy world or perhaps just a world of words. However, in this chapter, I want to go beyond that and look at some phenomena that are real but appear to be inherently non-understandable.

And by this, I mean that there are phenomena for which it appears intrinsically impossible to break them down into the nuts and bolts of something that is more fundamental. This is because there are no observable facts that relate to these phenomena; there are no nuts and bolts. And if something is inherently non-understandable then I suggest that it be given the label 'magic'. This is because such phenomena are beyond our comprehension in the way that the word 'magic' means 'beyond our comprehension'.

So what are these non-understandable and magical phenomena that are nevertheless real? There seem to be two distinct categories of this. One to do with matter and the other with consciousness.

The first is the fact that our physical universe exists. Or to put it another way: something exists instead of nothing. In this instance, 'nothing' means nothing at all, no time, no space, no matter, nothing. And the fact that something exists instead of nothing defies explanation and is beyond understanding. One can only say that it is by magic.

Associated with this, but somewhat distinct from it, is the existence of complex molecules that enable the evolution of life. One could envisage, in terms of the first act of magic, that time and space and matter were created, but in a universe that was entirely bereft of life because the form of the matter and the forces between the elements of matter did not allow for the formation of complex molecules and the eventual evolution of life. In other words, not only does something exist, but it exists in a form that can create life. So the fact that such matter and forces and fundamental particles that facilitate the evolution of life do exist in our universe, is a second act of magic, for it is beyond explanation.

The second category of magic is that of the phenomenon of consciousness. Consciousness is non-material and yet it exists in our material universe. It is beyond understanding. It is magical.

I should note here that in Chapter 11: 'A Theory of Consciousness', I described how the phenomenon of self-awareness could be explained and understood in terms of how a logical brain can create a model of the world from its sense-data and then subsequently when that logical brain and its model of the world is sufficiently advanced, it can place itself within its own model of the world and hence achieve self-awareness. But this is only self-awareness and not consciousness, I only speculated that the phenomenon of consciousness could be emergent from that self-awareness, in a non-logical and magical way.

For consciousness is undoubtedly magical. It is a phenomenon, a personal experience that is entirely non-material and cannot be understood in material terms or indeed in any terms at all.

Associated with consciousness, but distinct from it, is the personal experience of happiness. This was discussed in Chapter 10: 'The Foundations of Reality and Purpose'; how an evolving logical processor requires a goal, in order to operate efficiently and make decisions within the world. For want of a better word I labelled this goal as 'happiness'. It is the goal to which we all aspire. But the actual experience of this phenomenon is beyond the mere consciousness that was previously discussed; it deserves its own act of magic.

These four acts of magic are beyond understanding. They are beyond physics beyond biology, beyond any academic discipline founded on the real world.

Of course, people can and do create fictitious fantasies that purport to explain these phenomena, but they are just a bit of fun and do not in any way constitute understanding.

An appreciation of this magic may be important for human life. It is an acceptance that there are things beyond understanding; things that give life that sense of wonder and sparkle.

Then the question arises where can an appreciation of this magic be found?

People may find the experience of magic in different places. For example, people might find a sense of magic in a glorious sunset, a rainbow in a stormy sky, in quiet reflection or with a group of friends. Or perhaps it could be found in a star-studded sky, in a flower, a colourful crystal, a seagull floating on a breeze or a cricket chirping on a still night. Or perhaps one might find it in a piece of music, through dance, the birth of a child or simply in making others happy.

While many people can live their lives quite happily without any appreciation of the magic of life, for others it is of paramount importance. The experience of magic can give one an appreciation for the wonders and beauty of life itself.

In conclusion, the magic of life is to be found in places that are beyond rational logic, beyond the world of words but rather in the pure experience of life itself.

Perhaps the most long-term aim, what some might call 'purpose', is to facilitate the long-term survival of life in general and the human species in particular so that others too can appreciate the magic of life.

*And so we have come to the end of our journey. We have come a long way since we started out when we had little more than a logical processor and some sense-data. As a species we have evolved to fit with the environment of the Earth. It is our birthright to try to make sense of the amazing world in which we find ourselves, to wonder at its mysteries and above all to enjoy our life's journey.*

# Glossary

**Abstract system:** System that has symbols, rules and axioms which can generate theorems but which have no direct link to the real world.

**Algorithm:** Precise description of a logical process that encompasses a number of rules.

**Belief:** An idea that a person holds in their head.

**Best:** Descriptor for the optimum of a number of possibilities according to specified criteria.

**Consciousness:** The experience of being alive.

**Disembodied statement:** Statement that has no discernible author.

**Evolution:** Process of variation and survival by which life evolves from non-organic matter.

**Fantasy:** Idea or set of ideas that are without an explicit link to the real world.

**Freedom:** State of mind in which one can make decisions based entirely upon one's model of the world and without impediment from other people.

**Happiness:** Goal or direction to which the brain aspires.

**Interesting:** Descriptor for an idea or theorem that has the potential to generate ideas that relate to the world of decision-making.

**Logic:** Process of inference using specified rules.

**Magic:** That which is inherently unknowable.

| | |
|---|---|
| **Paradigm:** | Collection of ideas with a common theme. |
| **Pattern:** | The final output of a pattern identification process and which can be used to recreate the original data. |
| **Philosophy:** | Branch of knowledge that encompasses all others. |
| **Real world/Reality:** | The world beyond our senses that we can only infer exists through the process of pattern identification. |
| **Rule:** | Specified instruction for the manipulation of symbols within an abstract system. |
| **SCALES:** | The criteria for a good philosophy: Self-consistency, Comprehensiveness, Accuracy, Logic, Explicitness and Simplicity. |
| **Sense-data:** | Information garnered from the senses. |
| **Standard Western philosophy (SWP):** | Predominant philosophy of the Western world that can be found in the philosophy section of a university library. |
| **Template:** | Possible pattern or seed used in the pattern identification process. |
| **The Pattern Paradigm (TPP):** | The name of the philosophy described in this book. |
| **Theorem:** | String of symbols generated by an abstract system from its rules and axioms. |
| **Truth:** | Label given to a pattern, idea or theorem that is considered to be the best one currently available. |
| **Word:** | Label for a pattern. |